Cashing In across the Golden Triangle

About the Authors

DR. THEIN SWE teaches economics, finance, and globalization studies at Payap University in the International MBA program and South East Asian Institute of Global Studies. He has served as Alternate Executive Director of the World Bank (1977–1979); Deputy Head of Mission, Vietnam; and Principal Portfolio Specialist at the Asian Development Bank (1990–2003).
E-mail: tswe@seaigs.org

DR. PAUL CHAMBERS is Research Director at the South East Asian Institute of Global Studies at Payap University. From 2008 to 2011, he was Senior Researcher at Heidelberg University. His articles have appeared in *Contemporary Southeast Asia*, *the Journal of East Asian Studies*, and the *Asian Journal of Political Science*.
E-mail: pchambers@seaigs.org

Cashing In
across the Golden Triangle

Thailand's Northern Border Trade with China, Laos, and Myanmar

by

Thein Swe and Paul Chambers

MEKONG PRESS

Mekong Press was initiated in 2005 by Silkworm Books with the financial support of the Rockefeller Foundation. In 2007, the Mekong Press Foundation was registered as a nonprofit organization to encourage and support the work of local scholars, writers, and publishing professionals in Cambodia, Laos, Vietnam, and the other countries in the Greater Mekong Subregion. Books published by Mekong Press (www.mekongpress. com) are marketed and distributed internationally. Mekong Press also holds seminars and training workshops on different aspects of book publishing, and helps find ways to overcome some of the huge challenges faced by small book publishers in the region.

ISBN: 978-616-90053-4-6

Illustration credits: Lai Jin Hui, p. 64; Jason Lubanski, p. 2; Jeff Moynihan, pp. 50, 55, 82, 108, 109; Prathan Inseeyong (Siam South China Logistics), pp. 75, 98, 111; Subantita Suwan, pp. 77, 78; Thein Swe, pp. 66, 87.

Published in 2011 by
Mekong Press
6 Sukkasem Road, T. Suthep
Chiang Mai 50200 Thailand
info@mekongpress.com
http://www.mekongpress.com

Typeset in Garamond Premier Pro 11 pt. by Silk Type

Printed and bound in China

5 4 3 2 1

Contents

CONTENTS

Tables and Figures

Tables

Figures

Foreword

I would like to congratulate Dr. Thein Swe and Dr. Paul Chambers from Payap University, Chiang Mai, Thailand on the publication of *Cashing In across the Golden Triangle*, which introduces their assessment of the impact of the new road networks in the Greater Mekong Subregion (GMS). The GMS program aims to develop the economy of the region as a whole. The development of the road network, which will connect the GMS countries at strategic points, is one of the program's essential sectors, along with electricity, communications, the environment, agriculture, and tourism.

This book focuses on the area known as the "Golden Triangle," which includes parts of Laos, Thailand, and Myanmar. The region is one of the centers for cross-border trade but, unfortunately, it has also historically served as a drugs crossroads. Since the end of the Indochina conflicts in the early 1990s, however, a major change has been introduced in the economy of this area with the support of the Asian Development Bank (ADB). As part of the GMS program, several important infrastructural and development projects are being implemented across the borders of these countries. These projects, naturally, have begun to produce positive impacts on local economies and livelihoods.

This book examines the border economy of northern Thailand, eastern Myanmar, northwestern Laos, and southwestern China. Its principal purpose is to study how this frontier trade is evolving, and to analyze the current obstacles and challenges faced by these countries. The authors' intention is to indicate means of improving border trade competitiveness to enhance mutual benefits for all the regional stakeholders. The book also examines the political economy of the nexus between state policy, border trade, and economic development. This is a pioneering assessment of subregional economic cooperation, using the northwestern region of the GMS as an example.

The GMS was conceived in the 1980s when the Mekong subregion was still suffering from political conflict. The idea of bringing all the Mekong countries together came closer to realization when Laos and Thailand agreed in 1986 to cooperate in the Xeset Hydropower Project in southern Laos with joint financing by ADB and the Swedish International Development Assistance (Sida). This positive move and the successful implementation of the project no doubt provided hope for postwar cooperation among the countries in the region. With ADB as the coordinator, GMS was inaugurated in 1992, only a few months after the Paris Peace Accord (October 1991).

The main objective of setting up the GMS was to ensure sustainable peace and stability in the region. It was certainly a unique attempt by the Mekong countries to join hands when they were politically divided and suffering from long-standing conflicts. It is important to note, however, that the GMS countries historically share common social and cultural values. This factor has provided a strong platform for their work together as a group. It has ensured the harmony that is essential for maintaining group ownership of the GMS program and its initiatives. The GMS program has in turn drawn the countries closer together and contributed substantially to the improvement of the investment climate in the subregion.

This book confirms that the subregion has evolved into a region, with increasingly closer cooperation in trade and development. Within the GMS, the North-South Economic Corridor (NSEC) links the growing economic engine of China with Thailand, Laos, and Myanmar via highways R3A and R3B, as well as the Mekong River. These linkages have led to burgeoning border trade and economic development, contributing to greater economic growth in the GMS. The GMS countries recognize the challenges which remain, such as improving customs efficiency, strengthening and enhancing the capacity of bureaucratic institutions, streamlining cross-border regulations, and improving infrastructure.

Through these measures, the GMS countries will achieve faster socio-economic growth.

The GMS projects will continue to evolve conceptually as well as take on new approaches. It is hoped that this assessment of the GMS program will be widened in the near future following the initiative taken by the authors of this study.

Noritada Morita
Chairman and CEO, Asia Strategy Forum

Preface

This study began in 2005 as an idea to try to understand Thailand's northern economy. It has since mushroomed into an analysis of Thailand's burgeoning northern border trade with Laos, Myanmar, and China. An early version of the study entitled "Political Economy on the Perimeter" was presented at the 10th International Conference on Thai Studies, held from January 9–11, 2008 at Thammasat University, Bangkok. An early version of the section on "Frontier Commerce and Sociolinguistic Challenges" was presented at the international conference on "National Language Policy: Language Diversity for National Unity" held from July 4–5, 2008 at the Twin Towers Hotel, Bangkok, under the sponsorship of UNESCO and the Royal Institute of Thailand.

Many people have assisted us in this effort and we are grateful to each and every one of them. A smaller number of individuals were instrumental to the project's completion. We would first like to thank Mr. N. Morita, former ADB Director of Program West, who wrote the foreword. It is indeed a great honor for us to have the "Father of GMS" writing the foreword.

We are also greatly indebted to Chiang Rai Chamber of Commerce Chairman Mr. Pattana Sittisombat, who graciously explained the trade in the region, and assisted us in so many ways. We would like to record our appreciation to Mr. Lai Jinhui, an International Business MBA graduate of Payap University and currently a businessman in Bangkok. Without Jin's help we could not have interviewed many Chinese respondents. Jin also saved us in Boten, Laos and Mongla, Myanmar, where almost everyone speaks Chinese. Mr. Samuel Dashi, a student from Myanmar, who is completing his International Business MBA program at Payap University, was also very helpful on the trip to Laos and Myanmar. Likewise, Ms. Aksone Saysana, a Laotian sociology student and researcher at Chiang Mai University, proved to be invaluable on the research trip to Laos.

We also wish to thank Achans Naruthep Euathrongchit and Pongthep Termsnguangwong, of the Faculty of Business Administration at Payap University. We gratefully acknowledge the assistance of: Martha Butt, Adam Dedman, Presert Jiachareontrakul, Khin Aye Than, Jessica Loh, Jay Lubanski, Jeff Moynihan, Ho Nguyen (of St. Mary's College in Maryland), Eva Pascal, Ratanaporn Sethakul, Rux Prompalit, (Chiang Mai University researcher) Samak Kosem, Sirilert Krasaechai, Somboon Panyakom, Somchai Sirisujin, Subantita Suwan, Tatikul Chaiwun, Wutthipong Chautrakul, and many of our colleagues at Payap University.

Our sincere appreciation goes to Warangkana Imudom from the Bank of Thailand's Northern Region Office for providing easy access to data and information on trade and other statistics relating to northern Thailand. In addition, we would like to thank Prathan Inseeyong of Siam South China Logistics for his help, especially on the Chiang Saen area.

We would not have been able to complete this work without the valuable assistance of Achan Tom Hughes and Dr. Tynn Tynn Sann who carefully edited our draft within a very limited time.

Last but not least, we would like to thank the many people who agreed to be interviewed, some anonymously, and who provided valuable input to this study.

Thein Swe and Paul Chambers
February 15, 2011

Abbreviations

ACFTA	ASEAN-China Free Trade Agreement
ACMECS	Ayeyawady-Chao Phraya-Mekong Economics Cooperation Strategy
ADB	Asian Development Bank
AEC	ASEAN Economic Community
AFTA	ASEAN Free Trade Area
APB	Agriculture Promotion Bank
ASEAN	Association of Southeast Asian Nations
BBT	Boten Border Trade
BCEL	Banque pour le Commerce Exterieur
BOI	Board of Investment
BOT	Bank of Thailand
CBTA	Cross-border Transport Agreement
CLMV	Cambodia, Laos, Myanmar, and Vietnam
EGAT	Electricity Generating Authority of Thailand
EHP	Early Harvest Program
EQJDC	Economic Quadrangle Joint Development Corporation
EWEC	East–West Economic Corridor
FTA	free-trade agreement
GMS	Greater Mekong Subregion
GPP	Gross Provincial Product
GRP	Gross Regional Product
IOM	International Organization for Migration
ITSC-UCC	International Trade Study Center of the University of the Thai Chamber of Commerce

JCCCN	Joint Committee on Coordination of Commercial Navigation
JEQC	Joint Economic Quadrangle Committee
KMT	Kuomintang
LDB	Lao Development Bank
LPG	Liquefied Petroleum Gas
M2M	merchant-to-merchant
NDAA	National Democratic Alliance Army
NESDB	Office of the National Economic and Social Development Board
NESDP	National Economic and Social Development Plan
NSEC	North-South Economic Corridor
OAE	Office of Agricultural Economics
ODA	Official Development Assistance
PAO	Provincial Administrative Organization
PAT	Port Authority of Thailand
R3A	Route no. 3A (NSEC via Laos)
R3B	Route no. 3B (NSEC via Myanmar)
SEZ	Special Economic Zones
SREZ	Subregional Economic Zone
SLS	Shwe Lin Star Tourism Company Ltd
Sida	Swedish International Development Cooperation Agency
TAO	Tambon Administrative Organization
TCC	Thai Chamber of Commerce
TDRI	Thailand Development Research Institute
TNC	transnational corporation
TWh	terrawatt per hour
UNCTAD	United Nations Conference on Trade and Development
UNESCO	United Nations Educational, Scientific, and Cultural Organisation
UNESCAP	United Nations Economic and Social Commission for Asia and the Pacific
UWSA	United Wa State Army
VPL	Vieng Phouka Lignite Company Ltd

VAT	value-added tax
WTO	World Trade Organization

Key Border Towns in the Golden Triangle

TACHILEK, Shan State, Myanmar, is the border town opposite Mae Sai, in Chiang Rai Province, Thailand. It has a population of about 100,000. Around 4,000 visitors, including tourists, cross over to this town each day via the Mae Sai border. Most of them are traders of gemstones, handicrafts, and other traditional goods.

MAE SAI, Chiang Rai Province, Thailand, is the border town opposite Tachilek as well as the northernmost district of Thailand. It has a population of about 60,000. It is a strategic border crossing between Thailand and Myanmar, given that the Asian Highway Network (Thai Highway 1 or Pahonyothin Road) crosses the Mae Sai River to Myanmar and then proceeds to southern China.

CHIANG SAEN, Chiang Rai Province, Thailand, is a river port and district on the Mekong River close to the Golden Triangle where Laos and Myanmar border Thailand. It has a population of about 55,000. Trade between Thailand and China here consists mainly of vegetables and fruit via the Mekong River.

CHIANG KHONG, Chiang Rai Province, Thailand, is a border town and district east of both Mae Sai and Chiang Saen. It stands across the Mekong River from Houayxay, Laos. It has a population of about 57,000. The Asia Highway Network passes through Chiang Khong through Laos to southern China. Thailand's border trade here consists primarily of wood products from Laos and consumer products exported to Laos.

HOUAYXAY, Bokeo Province, Laos sits on the Mekong River across from Chiang Khong, Thailand. Houayxay is the capital of this smallest and sparsely populated Lao province. It has a population of about 60,000. Houayxay serves as the official frontier point between northern Thailand and northern Laos. A bridge between Chiang Khong and Houayxay is currently under construction. The border trade is dominated by freight in transit between China and Laos.

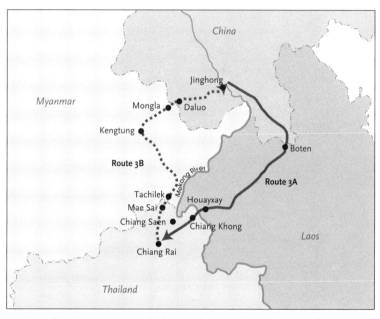

Map of the three NSEC routes. To the west is R3B; to the east is R3A; in the center is the Mekong River route.

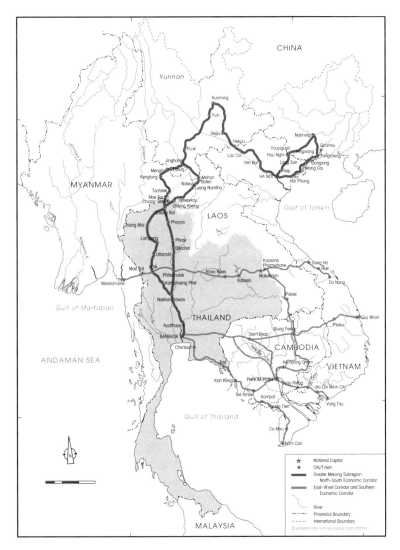

The GMS North-South Economic Corridor from Kunming to Bangkok
Source: Adapted from Asian Development Bank, http://www.adb.org/GMS/
Economic-Corridors/nsec.asp#.

Introduction

In July 1971, US Assistant Secretary of State Marshall Green declared at a press conference that drugs were proliferating through a "golden triangle" including Laos (the Lao People's Democratic Republic), Burma (Myanmar), and Thailand. In describing the region as a triangle, Green implicitly recognized the absence of narcotics cultivation in America's new friend, China. The region has long been known as a center for often nefarious cross-border trade and remains infamous today as a drugs crossroads.

Yet the definition of the Golden Triangle itself has often been elusive. Sometimes it refers to a wide, nebulous territorial swathe across parts of southern Yunnan in China, and the northern provinces of Myanmar, Thailand, and Laos. At other times it has specifically referred to a smaller zone at the confluence of the Ruak and Mekong rivers, and the juncture of the Lao, Myanmar, and Thai borders, 12 kilometers from Chiang Saen district. Sop Ruak village in Thailand has been the settlement closest to the center of the Triangle since the 1980s. Here a carnivalesque community has developed—complete with resorts, souvenir shops, a giant golden Buddha image, and the Hall of Opium—catering only to tourists. Today, the Golden Triangle has another meaning: the area where Chiang Rai Province in Thailand borders Myanmar and Laos. It is specifically the area within these parameters which this study examines.

The Buddha at Sop Ruak village in the Golden Triangle

Origins

The Golden Triangle has had a long, colorful history; it has been home to at least four different civilizations dating from the first century A.D.: Souvannakhomkham in present-day Laos and Nakhapun Singhanuwat Nakorn or Yonok Nakorn Chaiburi Sri Chiang Saen in Thailand. In the thirteenth century, these kingdoms were conquered and, along with Chiang Khong and other principalities in the region, were incorporated into the growing suzerainty of the Kingdom of Lanna under Mengrai the Great. Lanna itself eventually became a tributary state of both the Burmese and the Thais at Ayutthaya. During the 1870s, Siam began reasserting control over Lanna, encouraged especially by American missionaries and, less directly, the US government.[1] This led to a rebellion (led by the holy man Phraya Phap) in Chiang Mai in 1889, as lesser Lanna royalty, village headmen, and their followers reacted to Siam's centralizing and burdensome adjustments to Chiang Mai's power structure as well as the corruption of Siamese commissioners in Chiang Mai.[2] Yet the resistance was crushed and, in 1899 Lanna officially became part of Siam. In 1939, the Lanna dynasty officially ended. Today, the Na Chiang Mai family remains unofficially as the royal family of old Lanna.

Over the centuries, Souvannakhomkham disappeared in dense forest while Chiang Saen and Chiang Khong became important Mekong river ports. In the nineteenth century, both townships were right on Siam's northern border with French Indochina, while the nearby settlement of Mae Sai thrived on Siam's boundary with British Burma.

The Narcotics Trade

After the Communist victory in China in 1949, some of the defeated Kuomintang (KMT) Nationalist soldiers began settling on both the Myanmar and Thai sides of the Golden Triangle and initiated a lucrative trade in opium. The thriving trade that ensued coincided with, and was fuelled by, the Cold War, and the Golden Triangle found itself embroiled in ideological conflict across the Mekong basin. While the KMT were supported and controlled by the Nationalist government in Taiwan, its operations were covertly bolstered by the United States Central Intelligence Agency (CIA). In 1950–51, the Truman administration had the CIA prepare and mobilize a KMT force numbering in the thousands in an unsuccessful proxy invasion of southwestern China. The KMT then set its sights on a more permanent presence in the Golden Triangle region, becoming powerful principals in the opium trade. The Thai government profited immensely from taxing the KMT's opium caravans moving from Burma into Thailand as well as conveying the opium to Bangkok, from whence it was sold on the international market. By 1955, Thai police general Phao Sriyanon and the Royal Thai Police (which was equipped by the CIA) were lording over one of the most powerful drug transshipment networks in Southeast Asia.

Phao and his associates were forced into exile following a 1957 coup d'etat and in 1959 the production, sale, and use of opium became illegal in Thailand. Yet the Golden Triangle was a remote region and it was hard to quash the opium poppy "cash cow," which was earning profits for the KMT and Thai border police in the area. Furthermore, since senior armed forces personnel, police, and civilian bureaucrats were being paid to look the other way, the drugs continued to be shipped to Bangkok. This illegal trade was facilitated by the ferrying of food and weapons from Bangkok to Myanmar to the KMT by the CIA's Civilian Air Transport (CAT) planes, which flew back to Bangkok with narcotics, helping to finance the KMT.[3] In the 1960s, the KMT expanded its trade in opium and even diversified into heroin. In 1967, the KMT, a then-renegade drug peddler named Khun Sa, and the forces of Lao general Ouane Rattikone engaged in a battle to control the drug trade in the Sop Ruak village area.[4]

The CIA's involvement in these borderlands continued through the 1960s as the agency sought to build up its influence in the region and bankroll its local non-state allies. CIA support included acquiescence or even promotion of the narcotics trade run by the KMT and other groups such as pro-American Hmong (who were fighting alongside the United States in the "secret" Lao war). In 1970, 70 percent of the world's supply of opium and heroin originated from the Golden Triangle. Sop Ruak itself remained little more than a small village of farmers. Khun Sa came to dominate 80 percent of the Golden Triangle drug trade during the late 1970s and 1980s, and by 1990 controlled half of the global heroin trade. The US Drug Enforcement Agency (and other antinarcotics agencies) seemed powerless to apprehend him. Khun Sa became a legend as a global drug merchant, headquartered at Hin Taek, Thailand, not far from the Sop Ruak twin-river confluence.[5]

By 2007, Khun Sa was dead and the Golden Triangle was producing only about 5 percent of the world's opium, according to the United Nations Office on Drugs and Crime.[6] Afghanistan has taken over as the major supplier of the world's opium since the beginning of the war there in 2002, but the steep reduction of opium production in the Golden Triangle is also due to policy shifts in Thailand, Laos, and Myanmar (see fig. 1.1). The scale of opium trafficking in the region has accordingly waned (although opium poppy cultivation increased somewhat in Myanmar in 2007).[7] Although the drug trade continues at an unquantifiable rate, legal trade and tourism are currently stronger sectors of the Golden Triangle economy.

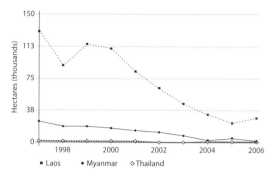

Figure 1.1. Opium Cultivation in the Golden Triangle, 1998–2006

Source: Based on information from Tom Kramer, Martin Jelsma, and Tom Blickman, Withdrawal Symptoms in the Golden Triangle: A Drugs Market in Disarray (Amsterdam: Transnational Institute, 2009), 22–25, available at: http://www.tni.org/report/withdrawal-symptoms-golden-triangle-4).

The Golden Triangle and GMS

Throughout its history, the Golden Triangle has been valued as a strategic crossroads. The end of the American-Vietnam War (April 30, 1975) and the Cold War (December 1991) brought peace to the area, providing a window of opportunity for these states to work together more closely. The countries of the Golden Triangle have come a long way since the early 1990s, when reforms and the notion of regional cooperation were still a hazy dream.

When the GMS Program began in 1992, relationships among the six participating countries—Thailand, Vietnam, Myanmar, Laos, Cambodia, and Yunnan Province (in China)—were still strained and bilateral trade was very limited even in the border areas. The GMS Program, with support from ADB and other donors, helps the implementation of high priority subregional projects in transport, energy, telecommunications, the environment, human resource development, tourism, trade, private sector investment, and agriculture.

As of the end of 2008, the forty-one GMS projects cost an estimated US$11 billion. ADB has extended loans amounting to US$3.8 billion; generated US$4 billion in co-financing for these projects; and mobilized a total of US$208 million in grant resources (US$94.1 million by ADB directly), to finance 179 technical assistance projects focusing on human resource development, tourism, the environment, trade, and investment.[8]

Regulating the GMS

Economic Corridors

One major focus of the GMS-driven economic development of the Golden Triangle area has been through the envisioning of the North-South Economic Corridor (NSEC) to promote trade and improve logistics.[9] NSEC involves three different routes along the north-south axis of the GMS:

- The Western Subcorridor: Kunming (China)-Chiang Rai (Thailand)-Bangkok (Thailand) via Laos or Myanmar;
- The Central Subcorridor: Kunming-Hanoi (Vietnam)-Hai Phong (Vietnam), which connects to the existing Highway No. 1 running from the north to the south of Vietnam; and
- The Eastern Subcorridor: Nanning (China)-Hanoi via the Youyi Pass or Fangcheng (China)-Dongxing (China)-Mong Cai (Vietnam) route.

The NSEC intersects the East–West Corridor at Tak and Phitsanulok in Thailand.

This book examines the western section of NSEC passing through the Golden Triangle, and explores its impact on the economy of northern Thailand (in particular, Chiang Rai Province) bordering Myanmar, Laos, and China. We compare the impact on the economy of the new roads and improved river facilities on the permanent border checkpoints:

- Mae Sai in Thailand and Tachilek in Myanmar;
- Chiang Khong in Thailand, and Houayxay in Laos; and
- Chiang Saen in Thailand and southern China.[10]

What role do local agents or institutions play in facilitating this burgeoning trade? How do state policies affect GMS commerce? To what extent has the GMS structure contributed to greater regionalism? We also explore the factors inhibiting this commerce, as a means of looking for ways to improve border trade competitiveness.

Beyond Existing Studies

The GMS may not be the first attempt at some form of cross-border regulation in the region, as Andrew Walker argues. The Chiang Khong Boat Operators' Association was a key actor in regulating riverine trade prior to the GMS.[11] Such regulation benefited the transport operators as well as local businesspeople, as the agents of cross-border exchange. But Walker's analysis predates both the accelerated decentralization in Thailand and China and the network of NSEC-related highways. Since our study focuses on Thailand, we need to take into account the impact of the growing disaggregation of administrative control on a provincial, sub district, and city level in the competition to regulate and tax the lucrative border trade.

For China, Kuah Khun Eng has pointed out that transformations in the border economy "can only be effected through an intricate compromise of the governments at the central, provincial, and local levels."[12] In times of peace, provincial and local governments tend to have more influence on policy, but when there is political tension, the central government looms large. Unlike the case of Thailand, he argues that China's central government dictates border-related policies, while provincial and local governments remain secondary players.

The question then may be how has the GMS spawned intensified regionalism. Xiangming Chen presents a rather rosy picture of post-Cold War global–local linkages, decentralization, cross-border social capital (particularly the role of Chinese socioethnic networks), all of which have been key to driving economic integration in Asia, including in the Golden Triangle.[13] Chen fails to mention negative aspects of this heightened regional trade, however, for instance, the surge in cross-border narcotics and human trafficking. Nor does his study look at the role of the state in regionalism.

Shalmali Guttal (2006) presents a more critical appraisal of the GMS. Guttal questions the extent to which state–state development has actually assisted local economies, especially since none of the official trade and investment agreements have been developed through the participation of local communities.[14] Guttal's criticisms about state-directed development in the Mekong basin are well-founded. Yet where regional cooperation involves states of such varying, if not vastly differing economies (for instance, China and Laos), the ensuing benefits and developments are bound to be asymmetrical. And, although state power in Southeast Asia has traditionally been, and largely remains, top-down, there are increasing signs in some Mekong states (in particular, Thailand) of greater local input in decision making.

Previous studies on the GMS are either in need of updating or do not focus directly on the subject of this analysis, which is Thailand's northern border trade in the first decade of the twenty-first century. This book aims to fill that gap, by focusing on the following questions. What factors have facilitated this growth in trade between the linked cities of Mae Sai, Thailand, and Tachilek, Myanmar, as well as between Chiang Khong, Thailand, and Houayxay, Laos? How has commerce from Chiang Saen, Thailand come to be increasingly linked with China? What are the barriers to border trade here? To what extent have national policies stimulated or hindered the ebb and flow of border trade? What is the character of tourism in the Golden Triangle borderlands? How have routes R3A and R3B influenced Thailand's northern border trade? How has Thailand's process of decentralization stimulated border trade in the region?

Following this introduction, this book is organized into twelve parts. Chapter 1 examines different theories by which to understand cross-border trade and regional cooperation, followed by our chosen framework. Chapter 2 focuses on Thailand's general role in GMS frontier commerce. Chapters 3 to 7 take a closer look at the NSEC highways and how they are transforming the physical and economic landscape of the Golden Triangle. Chapter 3 scrutinizes border trade from Thailand to Myanmar via the northern crossing at Mae Sai-Tachilek. Chapter 4 examines that route all the way through the Shan State to the Myanmar-Chinese border town of Mongla. Chapter 5 investigates the Thai-Lao border trade centered on the twin cities of Chiang Khong-Houayxay along the Mekong River. Chapter 6 explores this route through northern

Laos to the China-Laos border town developments at Boten. Chapter 7 looks at the river commerce between Chiang Saen, Thailand's major Mekong port, and southern China. Chapters 8 and 9 evaluate the relative roles of Chiang Rai and Chiang Mai provinces and their capital cities as rival northern Thai hubs of GMS trade. Chapter 10 turns the focus to how border trade and political decentralization have affected each other in Thailand. Chapter 11 investigates the ramifications of frontier commerce on social groups and languages mostly in northern Thailand, but also in the Shan State of Burma and northern Laos. The conclusion reviews the major themes and findings as well as proposes ways to overcome some of the obstacles to border commerce in northern Thailand that will benefit all parties.

I

Postclassical Realism and Subregional Economic Zones

How may we theoretically comprehend the new patterns in trade and development across the Golden Triangle borderlands, as well as the growing economic cooperation across the lower Mekong basin? Explanations may be found in liberalism, constructivism, neo-Marxism, neorealism, liberal-institutionalism, and postclassical realism, among others. In this chapter we will briefly examine these six schools of international relations to locate a tool that may be utilized to better understand economic exchange across these state boundaries.

Liberalism

Liberalism makes four key assumptions. First, nonstate actors such as multinational corporations and international regimes should be seen as political actors. Second, the state itself is not unitary: it is composed of competing individuals, groups, and bureaucracies. Further, military security is not at the top of the international agenda: there are a myriad other issues. Finally, interdependence is reshaping the world away from a traditional focus on state-centric balance of power issues.[1]

According to liberalism, frontier towns represent a nexus of abundant and profitable business opportunities. The eminent business guru and prolific author Kenichi Ohmae has been describing and applauding the trend toward an increasingly "borderless world" for two decades.[2] Ohmae contends that globalization is creating an unprecedented, borderless world that may well be bringing down both the nation-state (with its territorially linked economy) and the antiquated rules and practices of traditional, mercantilist economics.[3] Corporations (the principal movers in the global economy) seeking to maximize profits will have to diminish sentimental ties with the nation-states where they are headquartered and become more globetrotting. As economic integration spreads, trade barriers will diminish, and markets will expand, leading to greater growth and stability in peripheral areas.

The nation-state will be increasingly swept aside by the "region-state," which Ohmae defines as "an area (often cross-border) developed around a regional economic center with a population of a few million to 10–20 million."[4] Region-states "are such powerful engines of development because their primary orientation is toward—and their primary linkage is with—the global economy."[5] Trading nations such as Japan, China, India, and South Korea are increasingly pushing for the creation of a region-state across the Mekong basin. Nations on the fringes of the globalizing economy such as Myanmar and Laos are gradually opening up to liberalized trade.

Although Ohmae's vision of "region-states" replacing sovereign states in the global economy is breathtaking and ostensibly credible, the idea encounters problems. First, he never moves beyond ambiguous descriptions of it. Second, since he allows only for a maximum population of 20 million in a region-state, the GMS (with a population of approximately 325 million) cannot be included in this definition. Third, Ohmae never acknowledges the key role of central governments in creating and sustaining "region-states." Fourth, in a wider sense, he fails to credit states as crucial drivers of international relations. Fifth, he fails to acknowledge that the world economy is oligopolistic, not founded upon some "perfectly competitive model."[6] Finally, Ohmae sees the demise of nation-states as a foregone conclusion despite cultural distinctions and clashing nationalisms. Ohmae's visionary deep globalization, as with other liberalist analyses, is thus not useful for our study.

Social Constructivism

Social constructivism is a second approach that has been used in the study of international relations and organizations.[7] It holds that the interests of "agents/states"[8] are not given but socially constructed through their mutual interactions. Norms, identity construction, and shared values trump considerations of material forces such as interest-maximizing military arms races.[9] *Epistemic communities*—"networks of professionals with recognized expertise and competence in a particular domain and an authoritative claim to policy-relevant knowledge within that domain"—exercise influence over elite decision-makers.[10] Rule-governed cooperative structures, such as the GMS, can over time produce changes in state beliefs and values, redefining state interests and outlooks toward other states. The result can be habituated cooperation, and eventual collective identity. One can certainly argue that in the GMS, collective identity formation and building have begun to develop. Indeed, as Jörn Dosch points out, "epistemic communities have emerged among scholars of the six GMS countries (mainly, however, comprising Chinese, Thai, and Vietnamese academics)."[11]

Yet Dosch admits that since the GMS "does not involve the private sector and other nongovernmental [non-state] actors at any noticeable level," it becomes challenging to apply social constructivism to it.[12] Constructivists might also be criticized for offering an over-nebulous approach to international relations, given their emphasis on ephemeral ideas that are difficult to measure. The result is a lack of parsimony, which makes explanation—a key objective of theory building—much more difficult to achieve. Furthermore, in terms of predictive capacities, the ambiguities of social constructivism make this image "better at describing the past than anticipating the future."[13] Finally, for the purposes of this study, social constructivism fails on two accounts. First, institutions such as the GMS that may have been "constructed" have not existed long enough to really corral member-states into a collective identity. Second, there are several overlapping economic unions across the Golden Triangle (including ACMECS, the Joint Economic Quadrangle Committee [JEQC], etc.) and this generates confusion: Exactly which of these structures (in terms of collective norms/ideas) are influencing which set of agents?

Structuralism

A third framework that may be applied to our study is structuralism/
neo-Marxism. This approach, derived from a Marxist emphasis on class
analysis and means of production,[14] focuses on historically-evolving
capitalist relations of dominance and exploitation to understand world
politics. It presents a "dependency" vision of the world where the
economies of less-developed countries "are conditioned by and
subordinate to the economic development, expansion, and contraction
of the economies of advanced capitalist states."[15] Immanuel Wallerstein
describes a "social division of labor with an integrated set of production
processes" in which peoples and states are constrained and shaped by
the workings of the capitalist world economy.[16] For Wallerstein, global
capitalism, beginning in Europe in the 1600s, has spread throughout the
world into areas comprising the core, periphery, and semi-periphery.
The core engages in the most advanced economic activities; the
periphery provides cheap labor and raw materials; the semi-periphery is
involved in a mix of production ventures, acting also as a transshipment
point between core and periphery.[17]

Another highly influential figure in this field was Antonio Gramsci,
who developed the concept of a historical/ideological hegemonic bloc,
the method by which capitalism maintains control over society, not
only through violence or economic domination, but also by using
institutions, ideas, and social relations to achieve consent without
force.[18] Neo-Gramscianism meanwhile applies critical theory (another
variant of neo-Marxism) to the study of international relations as well
as the global political economy. Craig Murphy has argued that a
Gramscian "bloc," comprising elites in countries of the North and South,
as well as an "organizational bourgeoisie" in dependent less-developed
countries, has collectively maintained a form of global hegemony.[19]

Neo-Marxism would contend that the regionalization of mainland
Southeast Asia—in terms of such growth polygons as the GMS and
bilateral free-trade agreements (FTAs), must be understood in terms of
the regional structures of production, finance, technology, and the

commodification of labor, all of which are linked and determined by transnational capital and perhaps also held together by a hegemonic bloc.

Yet neo-Marxism has been criticized for being too deterministic and explaining all manner of sociopolitical phenomena in terms of the economic mode of production. Second, a rigid classification of countries into core, periphery, or semi-periphery leaves out economies such as that of South Korea or China, which have moved up the ladder toward the core. Last but not least, there is the question of causality: does economic dependency lead to economic backwardness or does such backwardness lead to dependency? Given such theoretical drawbacks, our study moves on to other explanations.

Neorealism

A fourth approach that might be used to understand regional relations across the Golden Triangle is neorealism. Neorealism is based upon traditional realism. Traditional realism holds that the international realm is anarchic and consists of states that are unitary, instrumentally rational actors competing against each other in zero–sum games, and place greatest emphasis on military security.[20]

Where neorealism departs from traditional realism is that the former emphasizes that international politics must be thought of as a system with a defined structure.[21] International systems change when the distribution of power among states shifts between multipolarity and bipolarity. Order occurs through a balance of power in the system. Neo realists would view regional cooperative entities such as the GMS as a sort of stage show with the member-states as puppeteers. For the neorealist, such state–state cooperation would be a short-term alliance, using self-help and balancing to maximize state interests. Neorealism does not recognize interdependence or globalization as phenomena that can transcend state capacities.

Critics of neorealism charge that it tends to be system-deterministic, failing to look at actors or events beyond merely the system and its state units. This approach is not useful for our study because in neorealism, states are not disaggregated to reveal how domestic/societal or economic units or factors might influence international relations. It offers no method for accounting for systemic transformations save for temporal shifts in the distribution of capabilities. Finally, neorealism does not prioritize a plethora of other important transnational issues (e.g. trade, health, the environment), instead concentrating on security.

Neoliberal Institutionalism

A fifth approach that is perhaps useful to our study is neoliberal institutionalism (NLI). NLI acts a sort of theoretical "bridge" between liberalism and (neo)realism. NLI, like neorealism, recognizes the anarchic nature of the international system but argues that realism tends to exaggerate anarchy's significance and effects. State actors prioritize positive–sum outcomes. Such absolute gains occur through participation in international institutions (rather than the zero–sum realist instrument of self-help) that are seen by NLI as coordinating international cooperation in a world of intensifying interdependence.

Institutions are defined by neoliberals as "persistent and connected sets of rules (formal or informal) that prescribe behavioral roles, constrain activity, and shape expectations."[22] In addition, they provide information, reduce transaction costs, increase credibility in terms of state–state collaboration, and establish focal points of coordination. Within institutions, states can address a myriad of issues, including security, commerce, environment, and health. In terms of economics, neoliberalism ostensibly favors reducing the role of the state in the market and promoting cross-border trade and investment as well as privatization, deregulation, and fiscal discipline to maximize profit and increase efficiency. Companies seek investments in states where resources to be used as industrial inputs (such as hydroelectricity from Lao dams) are accessible and labor is cheap. Institutions promoting neoliberalism include the International Monetary Fund (IMF), the World Bank, and the ADB.[23] Proponents of NLI have even stated that "state actions depend to a considerable degree on prevailing institutional arrangements."[24] Ultimately, NLI sees institutionally derived cooperation as replacing the search for order inherent in realist power-balancing among states. The World Trade Organization (WTO), the United Nations, the GMS: these would be examples of win–win institutional arrangements that could boost international cooperation, maximizing the interests of, and rewards for, member-states. In the GMS, infrastructure, cheap labor, and capital are connected together under a multistate agenda.[25]

Alhough NLI offers an insightful synthesis of liberalism with realism, its focus on institutionalism as a driver of the world system has been criticized.[26] With regard to the Golden Triangle, NLI pays insufficient regard to the agency of states: collaborative strategies in the region have tended to be driven by individual states seeking to enhance their power through nonmilitary means, not just through the vehicle of insitutionalism. As such, this study shifts to a recent strand of realism as an explanatory tool.

Postclassical Realism

The most useful tool for explaining regional economic relations in the Mekong basin is postclassical realism,[27] not to be confused with neoclassical realism.[28] Like neorealism, postclassical realism contends that international politics is highly competitive; egoistic states are the principal units of analysis; such states engage in self-help; and material factors trump ideas or institutions in influencing international relations. In a departure from neorealism, however, for postclassical realism states are "conditioned on the probabilities regarding security threats, not worst-case scenarios," as in neorealism.[29] Furthermore, "long-term objectives are not always subordinate to short-term security requirements" as in neorealism.[30] Instead states can make trade-offs. As such, postclassical realism, recognizing that the growing integration of global markets is crucial for national economies, postulates that states may trade off a degree of military preparedness as well as military and human security[31] if the potential net gains in economic capacity are substantial relative to the probability of security losses. This they do in four ways:

- by actively seeking changes in international trade patterns;
- by creating more efficient institutions to reduce transaction costs and better ensure property rights;
- by using economic leverage to secure supplies of inexpensive raw materials and other supplies from weaker states; and
- by reducing nonproductive expenditures to free up resources for economic advancement.[32]

The approach comes close to redefining security to encompass the external economic sources needed for military capabilities, thus creating a sort of economic security dilemma in which states build up their economic capacities to achieve instrumental goals.[33]

Three factors affect the probability of conflict between states: technology, geography, and international economic pressure. Technological innovation facilitates the extraction of resources necessary to enhance a state's security. Geographic proximity affects access to externally-based raw materials as well as the utility of using military as opposed to economic methods. International economic pressure is a key factor if states decide to influence other states through economic, as opposed to military, means. Postclassical realists posit that states seek to enhance their share of economic resources, and hence their power, because it provides the foundation for military capacity, and indeed economic resources can be utilized to influence other international actors.[34] Power is defined as *resources*: the combined "military, economic, and technological capabilities of states." This definition possesses an inherent tension between economic capacity and military security.[35] Moreover, in certain situations, postclassical realism sees a role for domestic-level phenomena (e.g. business associations, bureaucratic corruption, culture) affecting interstate relations. Brooks elaborates: "For postclassical realism, analyses should be undertaken in stages: first, at the systemic level, and then, if necessary, complemented and extended at the domestic level."[36]

Postclassical realism furthermore casts a spotlight on interstate cooperation, which it sees as becoming "feasible" if economic capacity gains outweigh "potential security risks." Indeed, developing countries may seek cooperation to enhance economic capacity (hence power) through participation in international institutions where such institutions can:

- enhance negotiating power vis-à-vis powerful economic actors;
- provide alternative export partners if other markets become protectionist;
- increase the chance of foreign investment, thus strengthening economic competitiveness; and
- allow member-states to reduce transaction costs and utilize economies of scale.[37]

Postclassical Realism in the Golden Triangle

How might this theory be applied to the Golden Triangle states? China, Thailand, Myanmar, and Laos exist today in an hierarchy of asymmetrical economic interconnectedness. Postclassical realism sees China as an economic powerhouse across Asia and a country which, in the Mekong basin, has traded off short-term security goals in exchange for longer-term economic objectives, especially given that military security threats in this region are currently low. The approach views post-Cold War Thailand as a rising industrial economy and trade hub in mainland Southeast Asia. Myanmar is a state possessing a sizeable military but a fragile economy. Finally, in relation to her neighbors, Laos is a relatively small and weak state.[38] Farther afield, postclassical realism perceives states external to the region (e.g. Japan) as maximizing their economic capacities through extensive investments and involvement in economic cooperation ventures with the Mekong states.

It is essential for China, Thailand, Myanmar, and Laos to attract more foreign investment, diminish production costs, ensure a supply of industrial inputs, maintain economic output at full capacity, improve transportation infrastructure, and enhance their industrial processes to compete effectively on the international market.

Southwestern China craves a trade route outlet southwards across the Mekong basin to Bangkok or Yangon, and to markets further abroad. At the same time, such an artery provides China with a means of importing necessary inputs or products for its southwestern economy. Thailand requires cheap and plentiful labor and raw materials to augment its relatively strong economic position. Thailand's once antagonistic Mekong neighbors are now providing it with such needed inputs as well as markets for Thai goods. Myanmar and Laos can enhance their economic capacities by cooperating with China and Thailand, for example in regional organizations, foreign investment ventures, and by faciliting Yunnan to Bangkok commerce. Ultimately, "[a]s the competitive demands of the global economy propel the states of mainland Southeast Asia [and China] toward greater economic interconnectedness, so the pressures…to form new…relationships with central governments in neighboring countries have multiplied and intensified."[39] Hence, "states remain the linchpins of international economic and political cooperation…"[40]

Subregional Economic Zones

In postclassical realist terms, the efficient institutions created by states focusing on enhancing their relative share of economic resources (and thus their power) might be seen in the growth polygons or subregional economic zones (SREZs) of the Mekong basin. An SREZ can be defined as a transnational economic endeavor (especially where borders are contiguous) and may include industrial parks, tourist attractions, transportation hubs, other commercial areas, and education centers. They generally involve cooperation between parts of nations instead of entire nations. They bring a range of diverse political, investment, and regulatory structures to bear on any given economic activity. SREZs offer key advantages to the participating countries. Participants benefit from mutual economies of scale. Bureaucratic red tape is minimized with fewer labor and tax restrictions, hence SREZs can bypass the often slow pace of state–state regional trade cooperation and trade liberalization.

SREZs also avoid the difficult task of having to achieve consensus among many member countries (such as within the Association of Southeast Asian Nations, ASEAN[41]). SREZs may further act as an impetus to quicken economic integration at a broader regional level. Yet another advantage of SREZs is that they can help bring prosperity to peripheral areas of countries that might otherwise remain underdeveloped. Finally, there is the belief that such economic cooperation helps to foster interstate peace and stability.

Thailand is not new to SREZs. Bangkok has been involved in the partially successful Indonesia-Malaysia-Thailand Growth Triangle since 1993. Thailand has also supported the establishment of both an ASEAN Free Trade Area (AFTA) and the ASEAN Economic Community (AEC). Yet given ASEAN's sizeable membership, negotiations to implement AFTA and AEC promise to be quite slow and lengthy. On the other hand, the establishment of an SREZ to encompass all of the Mekong riparian states, which could only have occurred following the end of the Cold War hostilities, may be a more realistic affair.

Within mainland Southeast Asia, the two key SREZs have so far been the GMS Economic Cooperation Program (including the North-South and East–West Economic Corridors) and the Ayeyawady-Chao Phraya-Mekong Economic Cooperation Strategy (ACMECS, see chapter 2). These and other SREZs depend on continued liberalization and an acceleration in border trade in the Mekong region. Clustered cross-border areas along the Thai-Myanmar and Thai-Lao border act as strategic nodes of trade and development in the GMS growth polygon.

Limits of Integration

While postclassical realism helps to explain the phenomenon of expanding trade cooperation among the asymmetrical economies of the Golden Triangle, SREZs, of course, have their disadvantages. If the benefits of states participating in the zone are uneven, then enmity can arise, leading to the demise of the accord. Where SREZs exploit divergent factor endowments, it is particularly likely that member-states with less-developed economies will come to see economic cooperation as a form of exploitation of their labor and natural resources. Aside from relative state benefits, integration can also produce differential benefits for different social groups residing within each country in the zone. Such uneven social gains are exemplified in a zone's division of labor,[42] where the cheap labor of certain social groups (i.e. "exploitation of migrants")[43] in more peripheral, rural areas is harnessed. Social inequities are also reflected in the fact that dividends tend to concentrate in more centralized urban settings (despite moves toward decentralization, as in Thailand). These intra-SREZ disparities thus facilitate an hierarchy of affluence among states as well as within societies.

2

Thailand's Role in Regionalism and Border Trade in the Mekong Basin

In the past two decades, Thailand has pursued the goal of more open border trade via multiple and simultaneous regional and subregional agreements, including some entered into as a member of ASEAN. It has also initiated bilateral FTAs with various countries, most notably China, India, Japan, Australia, and the United States (the last of which has yet to be concluded). In 2001, the Thai government began to advocate "forward engagement," prioritizing greater interdependence among Mekong states, rather than demanding democratization or greater protection of human rights in the region. Two years later, Bangkok set in motion ACMECS, a putative free-trade zone consisting of Laos, Myanmar, Cambodia, and Vietnam (which joined in 2004) that would also help develop Thailand's more impoverished northern border areas.

At the subregional level, the ADB-funded GMS has pushed for expanded cross-border commerce between Thailand and her neighbors. Largely influenced by Japanese financing, the GMS is founded on a neoliberal vision of reducing poverty by boosting economic cooperation and growth in the region.[1] While the GMS seeks to draw investment to the region through linking ample resources to cheap labor and potential markets,[2] detractors would argue that such a neoliberal agenda increases economic disparities, enhances corporate power, and involves policies that exploit the poor.[3]

With several, often overlapping, regional and bilateral trade agreements in play, our study focuses on how increasing regionalism impacts on the northern Thai cross-border trade. It should be noted that while these agreements reflect an overarching economic interconnectedness, the individual countries have generally practiced trade policies that bear closer resemblance to an underlying state-to-state economic realism. A case in point is the evolving and significant economic relationship between Thailand and China.

In this chapter we examine the relationship between, and the impact of, Thai regionalism on northern trade by discussing Thailand's external trade; the GMS economic corridors; key trade agreements, including the Cross-border Trade Agreement (CBTA); the China-Thai trade relationship; and finally, two revealing aspects of this new cross-border economy: the importance of migrant labor as well as the boom in casino-focused development in the frontier towns. Given the trade focus of this discussion, it is important to briefly look at how Thailand's ongoing political decentralization has been creating the right conditions for the growing openness of the northern economy.

Decentralization in Thailand's North

Intensifying economic regionalism has occurred simultaneously with the ongoing decentralization of state administration and the empowerment of business associations. This has meant greater agency as well as increased potential benefits for local governments, politicians, and entrepreneurs.[4]

There is of course a difference between formal decentralization and the decentering of state power. The former alludes to the formal transfer of state authority and/or responsibility from the central government to (subordinate or quasi-independent) government organizations and/or the private sector.[5] Such decentralization can be political, administrative, economic, or fiscal. On the other hand, the decentering of power, a notion associated with Foucault, focuses upon discursive domination and refers to instances where attention swings from centers and centralized power institutions to peripheries.[6]

In Thailand's North, formal decentralization efforts (in all of its variants), amidst NSEC-driven economic growth has, to some extent, helped to decenter power. These state-driven phenomena have, to various degrees, enhanced local autonomy, which can be seen in terms of greater political and economic clout for local entrepreneurs (and their business associations) mostly in the two major northern cities of Chiang Mai and Chiang Rai, although there remain continuing or even greater inequities for the north's poorer populations.[7]

As Jim Glassman points out, such strategies have "largely been unsuccessful" since they have tended to accentuate uneven development between Bangkok and most other parts of the country as well as heighten social inequality.[8] Yet *tambon* (subdistrict) administrative organizations (TAOs), provincial administrative organizations (PAOs), and municipalities are becoming more important in local government today.

Nor has the decentralization been unequivocal, since the Thai government has sought to recentralize various aspects of power, such as the Thaksin administration's 2003 inauguration of "CEO" governors who took over many responsibilities for provincial administration, ostensibly to improve efficiency. The advent of the "CEO" governors policy and efforts by national politicians to wrest back power reflects a continuing struggle between center and periphery in Thailand.[9] Though a conscious state effort at decentralization has begun (in many respects) to shift power from the center to the periphery, it remains unclear to what extent the Thai government's formal decentralization policies have actually led to a decentering of power to localities.[10] Nevertheless, decentralization in Thailand has had an appreciable impact on Thai border trade with Myanmar, Laos, and China.

The GMS Economic Corridors and Thailand's External Trade

Two GMS "economic [land] corridors" cross and connect Thailand, China, Myanmar, Laos, and Vietnam.

The concept of 'economic corridors' integrates physical infrastructure facilities (e.g. road, power, telecommunications), links this to and supports streamlined policies and procedures (e.g. related to trade and investment, to minimize non-physical cross-border barriers), and facilitates the development and expansion of cooperation in production and trade centers and linkages across a geographical area.[11]

The completion of the economic corridors has paralleled the rise of China's trade with Thailand, Myanmar, and Laos as well as among the four economies in general. China-Thai trade has skyrocketed since the 2003 enactment of the Thai-China FTA, exceeding 1 trillion baht by late 2007. However, with imports of ThB564 billion from China to Thailand surpassing exports of ThB510 billion, Thailand had a trade deficit with China of about ThB54 billion in 2007 (table 2.1).[12]

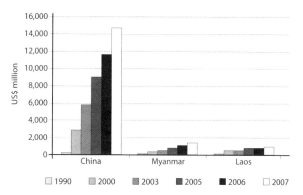

Figure 2.1 Thailand's Exports to China, Myanmar, and Laos, 1990–2007

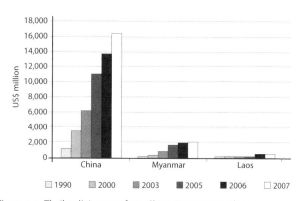

Figure 2.2 Thailand's Imports from China, Myanmar, and Laos, 1990–2007

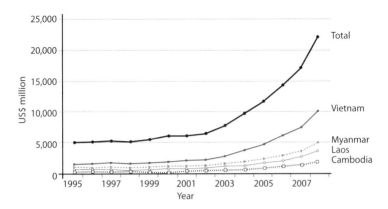

Figure 2.3 Thailand's Trade with Cambodia, Laos, Myanmar, and Vietnam, 1995–2007

Table 2.1 Thailand's External Trade with China, Laos, and Myanmar

	(ThB million)				
	2004	2005	2006	2007	2008
Thailand-China					
Total trade	615,317.48	816,322.18	967,501.90	1,074,817.39	1,199,413.44
Total exports to China	285,685.97	367,405.14	445,978.11	510,251.15	532,328.94
Total imports from China	329,631.51	448,917.04	521,523.79	564,566.24	667,084.50
Trade balance for Thailand	(43,945.54)	(81,511.90)	(75,545.68)	(54,315.09)	(134,755.56)
Thailand-Laos					
Total trade	27,993.28	40,090.57	58,473.17	61,479.15	78,828.33
Total exports to Laos	23,382.55	30,965.45	38,720.47	45,184.05	58,391.31
Total imports from Laos	4,610.73	9,125.12	19,752.70	16,295.10	20,437.02
Trade balance for Thailand	18,771.82	21,840.33	18,967.77	28,888.95	37,954.29
Thailand-Myanmar					
Total trade	78,849.47	100,295.63	117,556.90	113,073.61	156,228.52
Total exports to Myanmar	24,320.69	28,382.21	28,849.00	33,042.99	43,859.01
Total imports from Myanmar	54,528.78	71,913.42	88,707.90	80,030.62	112,369.51
Trade balance for Thailand	(30,208.09)	(43,531.21)	(59,858.90)	(46,987.63)	(68,510.50)

Source: Customs Department, Ministry of Finance (compiled by Bank of Thailand); http://www2.bot.or.th/statistics/ReportPage.aspx?reportID=52&language=eng.

Table 2.2 Thailand's Exports/Imports with China, Myanmar, and Laos (US$ million)

Year	Exports Total		By Country					
	Exports	%	China	%	Myanmar	%	Laos	%
1990	23,072	100.0	269	1.2	20	0.1	72	0.3
2000	68,964	100.0	2,806	4.1	555	0.8	419	0.6
2003	80,320	100.0	5,707	7.1	483	0.6	502	0.6
2005	110,160	100.0	9,105	8.3	777	0.7	846	0.8
2006	130,556	100.0	11,810	9.0	838	0.6	1,125	0.9
2007	152,460	100.0	14,834	9.7	1,055	0.7	1,443	0.9
2008	173235	100.0	15,976	9.2	1,449	0.8	1,933	1.1
2009	151972	100.0	16,076	10.6	1,694	1.1	1,801	1.2

Year	Imports Total		By Country					
	Imports	100.0	China	%	Myanmar	%	Laos	%
1990	33,414	100.0	1,107	3.3	49	0.1	40	0.1
2000	61,924	100.0	3,377	5.5	233	0.4	69	0.1
2003	75,824	100.0	6,067	8.0	827	1.1	94	0.1
2005	118,143	100.0	11,153	9.4	1,623	1.4	204	0.2
2006	130,605	100.0	13,801	10.6	2,136	1.6	476	0.4
2007	141,346	100.0	16,382	11.6	2,105	1.5	432	0.3
2008	178,526	100.0	19,935	11.2	3,447	1.9	569	0.3
2009	134,855	100.0	17,161	12.7	2,549	1.9	424	0.3

Sources: Asian Development Bank, Key Indicators for the Asia Pacific 2010, http://www.adb.org/Documents/ Books/Key_Indicators/2010/default.asp; "Country Tables: Direction of Trade: Thailand," http://www.adb. org/Documents/Books/Key_Indicators/2010/pdf/THA.pdf; "Myanmar," http://www.adb.org/Documents/ Books/Key_Indicators/2010/pdf/MYA.pdf; "Lao PDR," http://www.adb.org/Documents/Books/Key_ Indicators/2010/pdf/LAO.pdf.

Thailand's overall trade patterns with its GMS partners is charted in figures 2.1, 2.2, and 2.3. Table 2.2 shows Thailand's external trade with China, Myanmar, and Laos. Figure 2.1 shows Thailand's trade with Cambodia, Laos, Myanmar, and Vietnam (CLMV) from 1995 to 2008. Thailand has trade deficits with China and Myanmar but a trade surplus with Laos (table 2.1). Although China overtook Thailand as the largest investor in Laos in 2007–8, Thai investment in Laos remains high at ThB61.5 billion in 2007. In 2007, Laos had a ThB29 billion trade deficit with Thailand[13] that rose to nearly ThB38 billion in 2008 (table 2.1).

Finally, China became Myanmar's second largest trading partner and sixth largest foreign investor in 2007.[14] Thailand is currently Myanmar's largest trading partner (table 2.2).[15]

New Highways

The first route, the East–West Economic Corridor (EWEC)—Route 9—(initiated in 1998), stretches from Myanmar's port of Mawlamyine, through Thailand, across southern Laos, and ends in the port city of Danang in central Vietnam. EWEC benefits Thailand as a trade and investment passage to and from either Myanmar or Vietnam, as a means of collecting fees for traffic through the Corridor, and as a site for involvement in EWEC free-trade zones. The second route and focus of our study, the North-South Economic Corridor (NSEC), connects Kunming (in Yunnan Province, China) with Bangkok via one of four ways: through Laos (R3A), Myanmar (R3B), the Mekong River, or a combination of road and river. NSEC offers southwestern China, especially Yunnan Province, a cheap means of accelerating its commerce with the world, while offering Thailand expanded economic linkages with Beijing.

The first NSEC route is the 228 kilometer-long R3A from Houayxay to Boten; it is the sole sealed road crossing from China to Laos. Initiated in 1994, R3A was eventually completed in March 2008. The total cost of the project was US$97 million, co-financed by China, Thailand, and the ADB.[16] Laos provided in-country costs of about US$3.7 million via an ADB loan.[17] It remains to be seen whether Vientiane will be able to pay off this debt if the highway fails to generate sufficient revenue.[18] Laos's R3A has met stiff competition from the alternative NSEC route through Myanmar (R3B), which was completed in 2004 (see chapter 4).[19]

The final NSEC China-Thai trade route connects the port of Chiang Saen, in Chiang Rai Province to Guanlei, in Yunnan Province, skirting overland routes through both Myanmar and Laos. This is the least costly but most time-consuming route.[20] Table 2.3 provides socioeconomic details for the four largest Thai towns bisected by NSEC—Chiang Rai, Lampang, Tak, and Phitsanulok.

Table 2.3 Socioeconomic Indicators in Thailand's North

	Provinces along NSEC			
	Chiang Rai	**Lampang**	**Tak**	**Phitsanulok**
Area (km²)	11,678	12,534	16,406	10,816
Population	1,302,556	786,388	484,985	787,699
Provincial GDP (ThB million)	45,796	38,629	25,065	44,167
(% of Thailand GDP)	(0.64)	(0.54)	(0.35)	(0.62)
Per capita GDP (ThB)	35,149	48,983	51,868	55,936
(% of national average)	(32.04)	(44.65)	(47.28)	(50.99)
Daily minimum wage (ThB)	142	145	143	143
Labor (persons)	715,170	448,033	251,981	448,505
Share of Labor by Sector (%)				
Agriculture	(43.70)	(44.40)	(41.44)	(40.16)
Manufacturing	(8.20)	(13.72)	(7.53)	(2.47)
Services	(48.10)	(41.88)	(51.03)	(57.37)
No. of factories	1,735	1,642	510	1,322
(% of national total)	(1.41)	(1.34)	(0.42)	(1.08)
(National ranking)	20	21	54	29
Investment (ThB million)	5,642	53,020	9,734	9,552
(% of national total)	(0.14)	(1.31)	(0.24)	(0.23)
(National ranking)	45	16	36	37
Amount of BOI investments (approved) (ThB million)				
2001	20	45	0	48
2002	0	43	0	316
2003	171	60	0	268
2004	99	309	0	66
2005	342	40	435	119
2006	90	260	0	192
2007	230	227	0	576
2008	131	775	109	28

Notes: Population and labor data are from the fourth quarter of 2005; GDP is from 2005; the number of factories indicate those registered with the Ministry of Industry at the end of 2005; and the minimum wage is as of January 2006.

Sources: Estimates based on information gleaned from Thailand's Ministry of Industry, NESDB, and Ministry of Labor. See also Takao Tsuneishi, "Thailand's Economic Cooperation with Neighboring Countries and Its Effects on Economic Development within Thailand", IDE No. 115, August 2007, Institute of Developing Economies, JETRO, Chiba. Investment figures are from BOI (compiled by BOT).

In tandem with the expansion of the GMS highways, in April 2006 Thailand's National Economic and Social Development Board (NESDB) enacted the "Thailand Logistics Development Planning" to develop

Thailand into a regional logistics center. Thailand's total logistics costs account for 19 percent of the national budget with transportation accounting for 42 percent.[21] A major aim of the new blueprint was to vastly improve and upgrade existing commercial freight services.[22] In central Thailand, this included the continuing expansion of Laem Chabang port in Chonburi (the twentieth busiest seaport in the world) and Thailand's eastern seaboard as well as the completion of Suvarnabhumi Airport (perhaps the most bustling Asian airport) in Samut Prakan Province near Bangkok in 2006. Ultimately, Thailand is strategically positioning itself as a "Regional Logistics Corridor Hub…among the Indo-China and South China countries."[23] Besides Thai businesses, Chinese and Japanese companies handle the lion's share of logistics infrastructure across NSEC. And, according to Kevin Rosier, US Vice Consul in Chiang Mai, Thailand, "there is space for US companies."[24]

In 2004, NESDB commenced 35 programs and 112 projects (US$475 million) to be spread specifically among the key border towns of Mae Sai, Chiang Saen, and Chiang Khong, all in Chiang Rai Province, to be carried out from 2006 to 2014.[25] For Mae Sai, two customs offices and two border bridges were to be constructed (see chapter 4). For Chiang Saen, the current pier (built in 2004) was already being renovated while the customs office was to be enlarged. Meanwhile, a second port is being constructed (see chapter 7).

In Chiang Khong, the pier and customs office are to be fully renovated. Meanwhile, the third Mekong Friendship Bridge is to be constructed near Chiang Khong (the first connects Nong Khai, Thailand to Vientiane, Laos while the second links Mukdahan, Thailand to Savannakhet, Laos).[26] In addition, a Thai-Chinese international logistics center is being established in Chiang Khong. Furthermore, Bangkok intends to establish special economic zones (SEZs) in Mae Sai, Chiang Saen, and Chiang Khong.

Thailand and her GMS neighbors have also worked toward a one-stop customs policy.[27] Thailand commenced in July 2001 by establishing single-window inspections at major border checkpoints, whereby all inspection and paperwork is handled at one place and one time at each checkpoint.[28] In July 2005, the GMS countries agreed to sign the Cross-Border Transport Agreement, which was finalized in 2007. Full GMS-wide implementation has yet to be realized since each country has to adjust its regulations and procedures.[29] The CBTA, which was set to take effect in 2010, seeks to standardize traffic and customs procedures among all countries and initiate single-stop inspections at GMS border crossings to reduce transport time. For traffic from Kunming to Bangkok, the goal would be to reduce the usual five-day trip to twenty hours.[30] The fact that Mae Sai is among the "first step" border towns (these will pilot the CBTA) while Chiang Khong is a "second step" frontier city, gives Mae Sai a chance to offer a faster route to China and a potential edge on its NSEC rival. It also offers Myanmar potentially greater leverage over Laos (at least initially) in the race to dominate the middle leg of the NSEC.[31]

The River Route

Another landmark agreement was signed in April 2000, after four years of negotiations, between China, Laos, Myanmar, and Thailand: the Upper Mekong Commercial Navigation Agreement allows for the free passage of commercial ships between the ports of Guanlei, China and Luang Prabang, Laos. Officially inaugurated in June 2001, the pact has led to an almost immediate boom in riverine trade (see box).

As part of the pact, fifty-one reefs and shoals in the Upper Mekong will be dynamited to allow the passage of ships of up to 500 tons from Yunnan Province to Luang Prabang. This project, costing US$5.3 million, is entirely funded by China.[32]

Indeed, "the value of trade in the Thai ports more than doubled, from US$43.21 million in 2000 to US$87.85 million in 2001."[33] Business associations in the four signatory countries also established the JEQC in October 2000 to promote trade, investment, and transportation. The Committee holds exchanges among the chambers of commerce of the member-states, and is working to improve Kunming to Bangkok transport links. The JEQC also promotes business clustering among its members.[34]

The Agreement on Commercial Navigation on the Lancang–Mekong River

Signed by representatives of China, Thailand, Myanmar, and Laos on April 20, 2000 and official navigation commenced on June 22, 2001.

Objectives

To promote transportation along the river, facilitate trade and tourism, and strengthen cooperation in commercial navigation. As such, no charges were to be levied upon vessels of signatory parties by reason only of their passage through the territory of other contracting parties except only as payment for specific services rendered to the vessel.

14 ports designated under the agreement:

China: Simao, Jinghong, Menghan, and Guanlei
Lao PDR: Ban Sia, Xiengkok, Muangmom, Ban Khouane, Houayxay, and Luang Prabang
Myanmar: Wang Seng, Wang Pong
Thailand: Chiang Saen, Chiang Khong

Stipulations

- Most-favored nation status
- Respect of national laws
- Recognition of certificates
- Assistance for ships in distress
- Prohibition of dangerous cargo
- Recognition of environmental concerns
- Establishment of a Joint Coordinating Committee of Commercial Navigation (JCCCN) to manage transportation maintenance and consider joint regulations.

As with the CBTA, this pact exemplifies the ability of individual nation-states—implementing policies designed to promote national interests—to jointly pursue mutual gains and thus advance regional integration. Once again, state interest seems to have trumped the role of international regimes in enhancing regional cooperation. At the same time, both the CBTA and JEQC were implemented at the very least under the urging of the GMS.

Twinned Border Towns and SEZS

Under ACMEC's vision for developing the impoverished North, growth would be facilitated by the twinning of Thai border cities through improved transportation linkages with communities across Thailand's borders with its neighbours (e.g. Myawaddy in Myanmar and Mae Sot in Thailand).[35] In the North, this border twinning has concentrated on two towns on the NSEC routes 3B and 3A, respectively: Mae Sai (whose partner town is Tachilek) and Chiang Khong (Houayxay).

These twinned border towns represent parallel nodes in two transportation linkages connecting the Chinese and Thai economies through NSEC. At the same time, Thailand expects to increase two-way trade value by 50 percent among all the ACMECS countries. As part of ACMECS, Thailand's Bureau of Border Trade and Special Initiatives has already reduced border trade tariffs to zero on eight agricultural products, including corn, soybeans, and eucalyptus.[36]

Meanwhile, in early 2000, the Thai government also championed the Chiang Rai Border Economic Zone (the country's first special economic zone) as a business hub to promote commercial and industrial infrastructure in Chiang Rai Province as well as to strengthen trade ties between Thailand's North and Myanmar, China, and Laos along NSEC.[37] With ten border towns shared across the Thai-Lao, Thai-Myanmar and (indirectly) Thai-China frontiers (as well as a provincial capital to act as Thailand's regional trade nexus node), Thailand's central government granted Chiang Rai an initial trade budget of ThB10 million.[38]

The Chiang Rai SEZ was in line with the Thai government's growing push for industrial decentralization in provincial Thailand. Indeed, the Sixth and Seventh NESDB National Plans had putatively emphasized narrowing the disparities in economic performance between Bangkok and the rest of the country. In line with this objective, Thailand's Board of Investment (BOI) implemented measures to enhance industrial decentralization by splitting the country into three zones. While projects in Bangkok were considered to be in Zone 1, projects located in Zone 2 were in provinces just outside of Bangkok and received greater state-backed incentives than projects in Bangkok. Meanwhile, the lion's share of incentives were retained for provinces in Zone 3, the areas 150 kilometers or more from Bangkok. To further promote industrial decentralization, the BOI, in 1993, removed the requirement that foreign-owned companies in Zone 3 export at least 80 percent of their products.

These policies, enacted simultaneously with political decentralization reforms, proved quite successful in terms of attracting investment upcountry. Still, the strategies produced uneven development across different provinces, as hubs such as Chiang Mai and Chonburi received the majority of projects. In addition, industrial hubs tended to be situated near border zones. Despite these mixed results, the Thai state continued pushing the policy of decentralizing industrialization.[39] As Glassman has aptly emphasized, this was also an intentional "low-road accumulation strategy" that prioritized the relocation of investments to areas with cheaper infrastructure, real estate, and labor to maximize profitability for Bangkok-centered growth.[40]

Thailand and China

China has become one of Thailand's principal trading partners. Under the initial "early harvest" stage of their FTA, Thailand and China agreed that tariffs on more than 200 kinds of fruit and vegetables would be reduced to zero.[41] Thailand would export tropical fruits to China while Chinese winter fruits would be eligible for the zero-tariff deal. Yet hopes of mutually beneficial arrangements quickly disappeared with many Thai commentators saying that Thailand had received a bad deal. One Thai assessment stated that the early harvest agreement had only managed "to wipe out northern Thai producers of garlic and red onions and to cripple the sale of temperate fruit and vegetables from the Royal projects."[42] Data from Thailand's Office of Agricultural Economics (OAE) indicates that Thai garlic production dropped off from 2002 (125,000 tons/year) until 2007 (75,000 tons/year). Although there is no conclusive evidence, these numbers suggest that the 2003 Thai-China FTA (or the anticipation of it by farmers who then planted different crops) may have negatively influenced Thai garlic growers.[43]

The Thai media have also highlighted the fact that unlike their Thai counterparts, officials in southern China are refusing to bring down tariffs as stipulated in the reciprocal agreement.[44] Under the Thai-China FTA, import tariffs on agricultural goods were cut to zero in 2007 while China has continued its VAT surcharge at 13 percent.[45] While China's VAT has irritated Thai agro-producers, both foreign and domestic producers have to pay it and thus it does not merely discriminate nationally. Indeed, this potentially makes it more attractive to produce for Thai markets as opposed to Chinese. There have also been complaints in Thailand too about Chinese non-tariff barriers, including different trade regulations and procedures in different provinces of China. Other factors have, of course, hindered Thai agro-producers from competing with Chinese producers, including production costs for high quality items; upriver as opposed to downriver transportation costs; and China's control over water levels and navigability on the Mekong via its upsream dams.

Parallel to the Thai-China FTA is the ASEAN-China Free Trade Agreement (ACFTA). ACFTA was initialized on November 4, 2002, when Chinese Premier Zhu Rongji and leaders of the ASEAN nations signed the Framework Agreement on ASEAN-China Comprehensive Economic Cooperation. The free-trade zone was to take effect in 2010, with the four newest ASEAN members—Cambodia, Myanmar, Laos, Vietnam (CMLV) joining in 2015. The Agreement on Trade in Goods of ACFTA was implemented in July 2005, resulting in lower tariffs on more than 7,000 ASEAN and Chinese products. Two-way trade shot up by 23.4 percent in 2006, reaching US$160.8 billion.

In 2007, China and ASEAN signed an agreement on Trade in Services, which would expand trade in the ACFTA even further.[46] Exports from both sides were set to grow by 50 percent by 2010.[47] Like the Thai-China FTA, ACFTA has an "early harvest" program (EHP) whereby "ASEAN and China will progressively eliminate tariffs on selected products even before ACFTA is fully effective. Therefore, the package will presumably provide the incentives to accelerate the establishment of the ACFTA."[48]

Thailand is spearheading both the ACFTA and EHP, having already withdrawn together with China all taxes on 188 varieties of fruit and vegetables. Thus, "from January to June 2004, the Thai exports of fruit and vegetables to China increased more than 30 percent to reach US$210 million, accounting for 64 percent of ASEAN's total exports to China."[49]

The completion of highways between Thailand and China via Myanmar and Laos as well as the blasting of shoals and rapids in the upper Mekong River will boost trade between the two countries. Paiboon Ponsuwanna, chairman of the Food Processing Industry Club of the Federation of Thai Industries said "the road should facilitate export growth from Thailand to China by 5–10 percent. River transportation, which forms a major network in China, is more expensive and more time-consuming."[50] Still, other Thai and Chinese businesspeople see the river as a more beneficial route (see chapter 7).

Though NSEC is a GMS project, its origins trace back to a suggestion by Deng Xiaoping that China must find a "New Silk Road" southwards with a sea exit. While Beijing initially looked to the Gulf of Martaban in Myanmar, Zhu Rongji was responsible for shifting China's focus to Thailand, as he thought it would be much more difficult to cut through the Salween River basin.[51]

China's growing linkages with Thailand and ASEAN have grown out of three factors: ASEAN's closer orientation toward China following the 1997 financial crisis; China's own Great Western Development Strategy (GWSD); and Beijing's conscious postclassical realist effort to expand linkages with its southwestern neighbors to increase access to resources. The 1997 financial crisis demonstrated that an Asian bloc centered on China's massive economic engine could perhaps boost the region's economies, ensuring that any future economic crisis would be less catastrophic. Post-crisis, China's economy and clout in the Mekong basin swelled as that of other powerful Asian economies diminished. Since 2002, China has offered assistance, tariff exemptions, and different forms of debt forgiveness to the CLMV countries.

The GWSD was a policy implemented by the Chinese government in 2000 to promote the economy of the country's less-developed western region. Six provinces and five autonomous regions were specifically targeted, including Yunnan Province and Guangxi Autonomous Region, both members of the GMS program.[52] Major components of this strategy include the building of infrastructure (e.g. hydropower dams), attracting foreign investment, improving education (including the teaching of Thai language), and the boosting of regional trade (taking an active part in promoting NSEC).[53] Trade access through Bangkok gives western China a closer trade link than sending or receiving goods to the outside world via coastal eastern China.

Meanwhile, China's surging economy has fuelled its need for industrial inputs, markets, and logistics corridors, including a southern trade outlet to the sea. This has given rise to Chinese financial support for the construction of the four China-oriented corridors within the GMS: China-Vietnam, China-Myanmar, China-Laos-Thailand, and China-Myanmar-Thailand. The final two aforementioned routes form the eastern and western legs of NSEC.

Reflecting a postclassical realist foreign policy that encourages GMS integration in tandem with a national quest for resources and markets, Beijing has engaged in an adroit policy of playing each route off the others as a means of counterbalancing her southern neighbors so as to obtain the best deal.

Japan is the largest aid donor for CLMV countries. Its Official Development Assistance (ODA) supports a plethora of infrastructure development throughout the region. Japan is also the largest provider of funds for the GMS program. In 2005, Japan, seeking to counter the rise of China in the region, offered a new assistance program for CLMV countries.[54]

Beyond Japan and China, Vietnam is becoming an important regional economic player. While political and economic malaise continues to trouble Thailand, Vietnam's stability and rapidly growing economy is attracting growing foreign investment.[55] One report has predicted that "Vietnam will undoubtedly overtake Thailand in export value within the next 14 years."[56] However, Vietnam's economic outlook has not been so rosy recently and for all 2008, inflation is forecast at 25 percent.[57]

The Casinofication of the Frontier

Beyond subregional agreements, yet another phenomenon is energizing the Golden Triangle economies—casinos. Indeed, an argument can be made that expanding market liberalism and open borders are encouraging the "casinofication" of frontier development on Thailand's borders. By this, we mean casinos established across the borders from Thailand since casino gaming is illegal in both Thailand and China. The ban on casinos in both countries has opened up a market niche for Myanmar, Laos, Cambodia, and Vietnam to draw in customers from these two countries. Even Singapore, Malaysia, and the Philippines are joining in this to compete with the Las Vegas of the East—Macau.

According to research in 2002 by Pornsak Phongphaew of Chulalongkorn University's Faculty of Political Science, there are compelling reasons for Thai casino operators to establish casinos abroad: police raids and, more importantly, demands for kickbacks from Thai gangsters. The study added that most of the border casinos take in about ThB300 million a month (and enjoy revenues of around ThB200 billion per year), most of it coming from Thai citizens (who make up 90 percent of the cross-border casino clientele.) Given such dividends, it is only natural that most of the major casino investors have been Thai. Moreover, as the casinos stand outside of Thai territory, the Thai government cannot tax them. As such, the study concluded that "cross-border casinos and gambling establishments have an overall negative effect on the Thai economy."[58] In recent years, China has also joined in the casino development investments in the border areas.

Overall, however, since the mid-1990s, Mae Sai-Tachilek, Chiang Saen (Sop Ruak village), and Chiang Khong-Houayxay have each expanded due to cross-border trade and growing tourism (including casino tourism). The result has been increased economic prosperity for these areas in general, though there have been widespread disparities in terms of the distribution of commercial benefits for social groups in all three hubs.[59] For example, local entrepreneurs have benefited much more than laborers, who have continued to be marginalized. Nevertheless, the figures below reflect a positive overall trend. Table 2.4 illustrates

Thailand's border trade patterns with Myanmar, Laos, and southern China (Yunnan) from 2004 to 2008. Table 2.5 shows Thailand's foreign trade through customs houses in the northern region from 2004 to 2008.

Table 2.4   Thailand's Border Trade with Myanmar, Laos, and China (Yunnan), 2004–8

	Unit	2004	2005	2006	2007	2008
Total Exports	ThB mln	17,306.3	22,410.3	20,447.0	23,233.1	30,547.0
	%YoY	(64.5)	(29.5)	(-8.8)	(13.6)	(31.5)
Myanmar	ThB mln	14,255.8	16,701.8	14,899.3	16,420.7	24,928.5
	%YoY	(106.9)	(17.2)	(-10.8)	(10.2)	(51.8)
Mae Sai	ThB mln	2,039.6	1,894.9	2,143.1	2,669.9	3,993.2
	%YoY	(31.0)	(-7.1)	(13.1)	(24.6)	(49.6)
Chiang Saen	ThB mln	197.1	1,368.6	1,220.5	883.0	1,716.6
	%YoY	(902.8)	(594.2)	(-10.8)	(-27.7)	(94.4)
Laos	ThB mln	940.1	1,633.3	1,439.6	1,218.6	1,972.9
	%YoY	(70.6)	(73.7)	(-11.9)	(-15.4)	(61.9)
Chiang Khong	ThB mln	643.0	1,059.5	984.6	760.5	1,451.4
	%YoY	(27.4)	(64.8)	(-7.1)	(-22.8)	(90.9)
Chiang Saen	ThB mln	269.6	521.8	404.8	277.1	326.7
	%YoY	(816.3)	(93.5)	(-22.4)	(-31.5)	(17.9)
China (Yunnan)	ThB mln	2,110.4	4,075.2	4,108.2	5,593.8	3,645.7
	%YoY	(-31.4)	(93.1)	(0.8)	(36.2)	(-34.8)
Chiang Saen	ThB mln	2,110.4	4,075.2	4,108.2	5,593.8	3,645.7
	%YoY	(-31.4)	(93.1)	(0.8)	(36.2)	(-34.8)
Total Imports	ThB mln	3,431.3	3,120.5	3,912.0	3,506.7	3,835.5
	%YoY	(45.4)	(-9.1)	(25.4)	(-10.4)	(9.4)
Myanmar	ThB mln	1,782.2	1,422.6	2,034.4	1,803.5	1,687.9
	%YoY	(83.8)	(-20.2)	(43.0)	(-11.4)	(-6.4)
Mae Sai	ThB mln	628.4	306.3	457.4	712.3	252.1
	%YoY	(155.2)	(-51.3)	(49.3)	(55.7)	(-64.6)
Chiang Saen	ThB mln	1.2	7.3	33.4	4.6	0.2
	%YoY	(-28.3)	(522.2)	(359.6)	(-86.1)	(-95.9)
Laos	ThB mln	407.3	593.5	788.0	710.0	785.1
	%YoY	(34.7)	(45.7)	(32.8)	(-9.9)	(10.6)
Chiang Khong	ThB mln	295.3	451.9	680.2	614.3	619.2
	%YoY	(55.8)	(53.1)	(50.5)	(-9.7)	(0.8)
Chiang Saen	ThB mln	59.2	47.0	22.2	17.4	24.6
	%YoY	(-27.4)	(-20.6)	(-52.9)	(-21.4)	(40.9)
China (Yunnan)	ThB mln	1,241.8	1,104.4	1,089.6	993.2	1,362.5
	%YoY	(14.2)	(-11.1)	(-1.3)	(-8.8)	(37.2)

Table 2.4   continued

Chiang Saen	ThB mln	1,241.8	1,104.4	1,089.6	993.2	1,362.5
	%YoY	(14.2)	(-11.1)	(-1.3)	(-8.8)	(37.2)
Trade Value	ThB mln	20,737.6	25,530.8	24,359.0	26,739.8	34,382.6
	%YoY	(61.0)	(23.1)	(-4.6)	(9.8)	(28.6)
Trade Balance	ThB mln	13,875.0	19,289.8	16,535.0	19,726.4	26,711.5
	%YoY	(70.1)	(39.0)	(-14.3)	(19.3)	(35.4)

Source: Customs Houses in the Northern Region (Bank of Thailand, Northern Office)

Table 2.5   Thailand's Foreign Trade through Customs Houses in Northern Region, 2004–8 (ThB million)

		2004	2005	2006	2007	2008
1	Total Exports	86,789.5	98,739.5	100,968.6	87,491.0	92,099.8
2	Chiang Mai Airport Customs House	69,483.2	76,329.3	80,521.5	64,182.5	61,552.8
3	Chiang Mai Airport Customs Service Subdivision	5,709.7	7,842.1	6,161.7	4,255.3	1,251.8
4	Lamphun Customs Service Subdivision	63,773.5	68,487.2	74,359.8	59,927.2	60,300.9
5	Border Trade	17,306.3	22,410.3	20,447.0	23,308.5	30,547.0
6	Myanmar	14,255.8	16,701.8	14,899.3	16,420.7	24,928.4
7	Laos	940.1	1,633.3	1,439.6	1,294.0	1,972.8
8	China (Yunnan)	2,110.4	4,075.2	4,108.2	5,593.8	3,645.7
9	Total Imports	54,584.8	61,809.4	65,884.8	53,881.5	53,984.7
10	Chiang Mai Airport Customs House	51,153.5	58,688.9	61,972.9	50,141.9	50,149.2
11	Chiang Mai Airport Customs Service Subdivision	695.6	1,041.2	2,685.1	2,488.6	8,894.4
12	Lamphun Customs Service Subdivision	50,457.9	57,647.7	59,287.8	47,653.3	41,254.7
13	Border Trade	3,431.3	3,120.5	3,912.0	3,739.5	3,835.5
14	Myanmar	1,782.2	1,422.6	2,034.4	1,803.5	1,687.9
15	Laos	407.3	593.5	788.0	942.9	785.1
16	China (Yunnan)	1,241.8	1,104.4	1,089.6	993.2	1,362.4
17	Trade Balance	32,204.7	36,930.1	35,083.7	33,609.5	38,115.1
18	Trade Value	141,374.2	160,549.0	166,853.4	141,372.5	146,084.5

Source: Customs Houses in the Northern Region, Customs Department, Ministry of Finance

Labor Migration to Thailand

Regional labor migration, especially from Myanmar, has played a key role in the growth of Thailand's labor-intensive economy.[60] Although this volume remains focused on trade, it is necessary to point out that foreign labor has been crucial to the Thai economy for several reasons. First, the Thai labor force is currently not growing fast enough to meet domestic labor needs. Second, migrants from Myanmar tend to be willing to work in occupations that Thais find undesirable. Many Thais can afford to avoid such work given rising domestic salaries vis-à-vis that of migrants. Third, it is cheaper to hire Myanmar workers than Thais. "Thai employers often pay Burmese migrants 60–70 percent of the wages paid to Thai citizens."[61] Finally, the population of migrant workers from Myanmar is sizeable relative to other workers from abroad. Recent estimates speculate that up to two million Burmese migrants live and work in Thailand.[62] Besides Myanmar, migrant laborers also hail from Laos, Cambodia, China, and Vietnam. The majority of migrant labor in Thailand is employed in Thailand's fisheries, agriculture, manufacturing, construction, and service sectors.

In northern Thailand, Burmese labor has been essential to the local economy. "Numerous factories have been built in border areas, such as in the Golden Triangle frontier to profit from cheap foreign labor…[and] a longtime absence of official labour migration channels has resulted in widespread human trafficking and smuggling."[63] For instance, according to Yongyuth Chalamwong, research director of the Thailand Development Research Institute (TDRI), almost all factories in Tak Province shut down in late 1999 due to a labor shortage as a result of the government's deportation of Myanmar workers.[64] Also, in Chiang Rai Province's Mae Sot district (which has the highest concentration of factories in the province), a 2004 study revealed that 70 percent of the district's factory workforce were Myanmar migrants.[65] The Thai Ministry of Labor in 2007 estimated that some 109,000 Myanmar migrants live and work in northern Thailand, a higher number than in any other region of the country.[66] The point is clear: northern Thailand and the Thai frontier along the Golden Triangle are becoming increasingly dependent on migrant labor from Myanmar.

According to the International Organization for Migration (IOM), three principal factors are driving migration in Southeast Asia. These are the following:

- The pull of changing demographics and labor market needs in many industrialized countries;
- The push of population, unemployment, and crisis pressures in less developed countries; and
- Established inter-country networks based on family, culture and history.[67]

Though a large percentage of migrant labor is drawn by these reasons to seek employment in Thailand and Malaysia, not all such workers are moving toward these destinations. Indeed, Laos "serves as a destination country for migrants constructing major infrastructure development projects."[68] Moreover, the unstable nature of migrant labor has caused it to be quite fluid, with labor groups moving to one destination for a time and then to another. The construction of the various projects related to the GMS economic corridors themselves have contributed greatly to the temporality and fluidity of migrant labor in the region.

Uneven Gains and Local Obstacles

The Thai-China FTA has given crucial impetus to the acceleration of integration across the GMS. At the same time, the FTA represents a policy driven most prominently by nation-states rather than by any Ohmae-esque region-state or pressures from local/sub national governments or groups. Yet this FTA, designed to lead to mutual gains by China and Thailand, has thus far produced disproportionate state gains between the two trading partners (China remains dominant over Thailand) and has left the other GMS states in a more peripheral position, while also, thus far, failing to offset the marginalization of certain social groups (e.g. Thai garlic growers, indigenous farmers).

In the case of Myanmar and Laos, the GMS promotion of "open" borders has ironically meant more opportunities for official and unofficial payments to state officials involved in cross-border trade.[69] These payments (including multiple tariffs and freight stops) constitute a substantial hindrance to cross-border trade in northern Thailand.[70]

3

Border Trade between Myanmar and Thailand at Tachilek-Mae Sai

Thailand was Myanmar's largest trading partner in 2004–5 with US$1.9 billion or 38 percent of Myanmar's US$4.9 billion external trade. The Myanmar-Thai border trade itself accounted for about 70 percent of the total trade between the two countries.[1] Myanmar's largest border trading partner by volume in the region is China, largely through the Kunming–Ruili–Muse–Mandalay route. In 2004, the Myanmar-Chinese border trade amounted to US$1.15 billion and both countries aim to increase it to more than US$1.5 billion in the near future.[2]

Most goods traded through Tachilek in Myanmar are transshipped from China to Thailand with a smaller proportion moving in the other direction, from Thailand to China. Mae Sai is the chief entrepot for the Myanmar-Thai trade in northern Thailand. Thailand's principal exports via the Mae Sai-Tachilek crossing are petroleum and the consumer goods (such as vegetable oil, monosodium glutamate, condensed milk, alcoholic drinks, soft drinks, and instant noodles) that account for one-third of the total Thai-Myanmar border exports (see table 3.1). Construction materials ranked the second most significant, with a total export value of ThB165.6 million in 2008. Notably, construction materials meant for the new capital, Naypyidaw, readily pass through Myanmar customs—without official checking or interference.[3] Other exports to Myanmar via Mae Sai-Tachilek include manufactured items such as car tires, car spare parts, medicines, and foodstuffs (including edible oil).

Exports from Tachilek to Mae Sai are dominated by cattle, garlic, women's clothing, fruit, and timber (teak) as well as wood products. A significant proportion of these and other goods imported by Thailand via Mae Sai originate in China, including processed food (such as biscuits) as well as produce (fruit such as mangoes and apples; and mushrooms); electronic goods (such as Nokia cell phones, DVD players, and DVDs); household goods (e.g. clothing, bed linen, small electrical appliances, and toys) as well as cheap toiletries and other basic commodities.[4] Other items imported to Thailand via Mae Sai include fishery products, snacks, and precious stones (see table 3.1).

Table 3.1   Top Ten Goods Imported/Exported via Mae Sai, 2006

Imports (from Myanmar to Thailand)	Value (ThB)	Exports (from Thailand to Myanmar)	Value (ThB)
Alcohol from other countries	119,509,000	Petroleum (17,364,000 liters)	345,442,000
Cattle (2,980 animals)	22,000,000	Corrugated iron sheets	226,616,000
Garlic	19,686,000	Alcohol from other countries	148,994,000
Women's clothing	13,397,000	Automobile tires	106,975,000
Fruit (fresh oranges)	10,882,000	Medicines	89,022,000
Tree bark	8,522,000	Cement	59,741,000
Unpolished gemstones	5,064,000	Cell phone cards	57,496,000
Flowers/grasses	2,000,000	Liquid petroleum gas	44,633,000
Used machinery	1,591,000	Automobile and machine parts	25,585,000
Other/miscellaneous	103,937,000	Other/miscellaneous	1,007,393,000
Total	**306,588,000**	**Total**	**2,111,898,000**

Source: Mae Sai Customs House, 2006 Annual Report, p. 12.

Fluctuations in Border Trade

The Mae Sai-Tachilek border crossing has suffered from fluctuating Myanmar-Thai relations over the past decade. Indeed, border trade, though increasing, has been stifled by occasional border clashes, closures, corruption, and customs hindrances (see table 3.3). According to one Thai source, border trade would also increase if Myanmar businesspeople did not have to worry about their own authorities while engaging in commerce with Thailand and the kyat was more stable.[5] These problems are reflected in Mae Sai's uneven customs revenues, for instance, from 2005 to 2006 customs revenues suffered a decline in terms of both customs duties and excise fees (table 3.2).

Table 3.2   Revenue Collected through Mae Sai Customs 2005 and 2006 (ThB millions),

Types of Revenue Collected	Fiscal Year 2005	Fiscal Year 2006	
	Value	Value	Variation
Excise taxes	66.24	28.9	-38.15
Customs fees	8.46	3.26	-5.20
Total	74.70	31.35	-43.35

Source: Mae Sai Customs House

Table 3.3   Value of Imports and Exports through Mae Sai Customs, 1996–2008

Fiscal Year	Total Value of Imports (ThB million)	Total Value of Exports (ThB million)
1996	29.70	1,635.12
1997	97.74	2,605.98
1998	202.43	2,095.23
1999	154.36	1,997.23
2000	48.95	1,937.23
2001	55.61	949.23
2002	91.22	1,049.47
2003	85.20	1,564.10
2004	498.39	1,915.42
2005	385.99	1,916.59
2006	306.56	2,111.89
2007–8	717.01	2,489.38

Source: Mae Sai Customs House

From 1997 to 2001, Myanmar closed off its border trade with Thailand on numerous occasions and for various reasons. First, in the late 1990s Thailand had adopted a taciturn policy toward her western neighbor and relations between the two nations soured. Second, Myanmar on at least one occasion halted trade to stop rampant smuggling. Finally, Myanmar sought to pressure Thailand to conduct trade in us dollars to bring more hard currency into Myanmar's crumbling economy.[6]

In 2001, there was a thaw in political and economic relations between the two countries and both Thailand and Myanmar agreed to increase the value of their border trade.[7] Thailand sought to ensure smoother border trade procedures and prevent smuggling while asking Myanmar to lessen restrictions on imported goods from neighboring countries so that the two countries could exchange a greater variety of products. At the Mai Sai-Tachilek crossing, which stayed open more regularly, commerce (both official and unofficial) began to grow, albeit sluggishly. To expand the China-Myanmar-Thai trade at Mae Sai-Tachilek and reduce overcrowding, Thailand and Myanmar in the same year agreed to build a second bridge over the Sai River for heavy trucks.

In May 2002, when all border posts were sealed off again on the Myanmar side, border trade through the Mae Sai-Tachilek checkpoint, which normally accounted for ThB20–30 million (about US$500,000–$750,000) daily before the closure, was reduced to zero.[8] Only after five months (in October 2002) did frontier commerce resume. After late 2002, Thai-Myanmar trade once again began to soar.[9]

Later, the countries agreed to expand their trade account to help improve overall bilateral trade. Thailand boosted its purchases of farm and fisheries products from Myanmar, which in turn increased purchases of construction materials from Thailand. In early 2004, R3B linking Mae Sai to Tachilek, Kengtung, and Mongla (all in Myanmar), and to Jinghong, China was completed—an asphalt, two-lane highway 275 kilometers long. This has resulted in the facilitation of Chinese-Thai trade across NSEC while allowing Chinese and Thai tourists to pour into the region.[10]

The construction of the sealed road has meant that a trip that took two to three days now takes ten hours.[11] The road is to be complemented by a railway which in Thailand would extend from Mae Sai to Chiang Rai, then to either Chiang Mai or Denchai and proceed to Bangkok. Though NSEC R3B was completed in 2004, transportation obstacles remain. Internal instability along the stretch of road, and hence, security remains one of the biggest challenges on R3B route of NSEC.[12] In October 2004 the Thai-Myanmar border was very briefly closed following a leadership change in Myanmar, upsetting border traders. Moreover, Myanmar began to slap heavier export restrictions on border trade in mid-2005. Thai merchants continue to complain about bureaucratic corruption, overtaxation, and unnecessary inspection stops along the Myanmar leg of NSEC R3B (Tachilek to Mongla).[13] Despite this, Mae Sai-Tachilek bilateral border trade reached US$57 million per month by 2006.

In 2006, the area between Mae Sot, Thailand and Myawaddy, Myanmar was upgraded into a border trade zone. Myanmar authorities promised to keep the two towns at least partly under the rubric of the formal Myanmar border trade system, along with Tachilek and other key frontier points.[14]

At the same time, the Second Friendship Bridge over the Sai River between Mae Sai-Tachilek was finally completed. It was funded entirely by the Thai government (ThB38 million on the bridge and another ThB12 million for a customs house and other buildings). Chiang Rai's provincial permanent secretary applauded the bridge's completion saying that it would "facilitate the importation of natural resources from Myanmar and the export of household products to Myanmar."[15] The head of the Mae Sai Customs House added that the new bridge would be able to carry the heavier trucks transporting Thai export items such as oil and other goods from Mae Sai to Tachilek, and continuing on to Kengtung, Mongla, and southern China, as well as to India.[16]

With the second bridge over the Sai River completed, Thailand projected a 30 percent increase in its exports across the border to Tachilek.[17] But the borders closed down yet again in August 2006 when another border incident caused Myanmar to temporarily shut all its frontier passes except one crossing into Thailand's Mae Hong Son Province.

In addition, in August 2006, a reshuffle of customs personnel at Tachilek, Myanmar had led to stricter rules regarding Myanmar exports. The new rules meant a sharp reduction in tax collection at Mae Sai, and Thai exports into Myanmar decreased from ThB155 million (about US$4.1 million) to ThB130 million (about US$3.4 million) per month.

CHAPTER 3

A close-up of the old border bridge over the Sai River

The Second Friendship Bridge over the Sai River

In addition, Myanmar authorities had been placing restrictions on the types of vehicles permitted across the new bridge at San Pak Hee, usually only allowing—giving no specific reasons—pick-ups transporting fruit and vegetables. Following a meeting between Mae Sai customs officials and their Myanmar counterparts, the officers at Tachilek agreed to consider easing up on cross-border trade restrictions. This apparently led to the decision to permit wood exports from Myanmar.[18]

In late August, with the frontier at Tachilek-Mae Sai again reopened, a Thai company, Siwa Company Ltd, began to import Myanmar teak into Thailand. (The export of Myanmar timber into Thailand has been controversial since 1989 as some Thai logging companies had allegedly failed to act in good faith with their Myanmar partners.)

The September 19, 2006 coup that overthrew the Thaksin government led to yet another border closure (of five days, this time initiated by Bangkok). At the same time, between mid to late 2006, border trade between Mae Sai and Tachilek was increasingly affected by inflation. To add to this, in November 2006, over fifty Myanmar customs officials were arrested for corruption, illegal trading, and tax evasion.[19] In November 2006, the Mae Sai district representative of the Chiang Rai Chamber of Commerce, Boontham Thipprasong, stated that Thailand had registered a huge Mae Sai-Tachilek cross-border trade deficit over the past five years, mainly due to the 2003 Thai-China Free FTA as well as new trade restrictions in Myanmar.[20]

The Mae Sai customs report showed that from October 1, 2005, to September 30, 2006, more than ThB2 billion in goods were exported through its checkpoints, an increase of ThB195 million over the previous period (table 3.3). Over the same period, ThB306 million of goods were imported into Thailand, a drop of ThB79 million from the previous year.[21] By 2007, however, trade appeared to be robust once more. In 2006–7, Myanmar-Thai bilateral trade more than doubled: trade grew from US$1.6 billion in fiscal year 2005–6 to US$2.4 billion in fiscal year of 2006–7. Indeed, Thailand was Myanmar's number one trading partner, and has—at least until 2009—continued to be so (followed in order by China, Singapore, India, Japan, Indonesia,

Malaysia, South Korea, Bangladesh and Vietnam).[22] However, China is set to be Myanmar's largest trading partner if current friends continue.[23]

Myanmar is not as important a partner in terms of Thailand's overall external trade (see chapter 2, table 2.2). Thailand's foreign trade is predominantly with Japan, followed closely by China and the United States, respectively. Amongst Thailand's nine ASEAN partners. Myanmar remains the fourth largest trading parter in terms of exports (US$2,813.76 million in 2010) and eighth in terms of imports (US$2,073.03 million).[24]

As mentioned, border trade has grown to be a key part (up to 70 percent) of the Myanmar-Thai bilateral trade (see table 3.1). The lion's share of border trade, of course, represents transit commerce from China and other countries (the true extent of which is difficult to determine) and was expanding partly because of regional trade processes set in motion by the GMS and other bilateral or multilateral regimes.

At the same time, Thailand (from April 2006 to March 2007) ran a trade deficit with Myanmar of ThB73.4 billion for the first time since 1988. In 2006–7 Myanmar's exports to Thailand were worth ThB81.6 billion, while its imports from Thailand were valued at ThB8.3 billion.[25] According to recent data from the Bank of Thailand (table 3.1), Thailand ran a trade deficit with Myanmar of ThB30.2 billion in 2004 which rose to ThB68.5 billion by 2008.

Various reasons have been given for the deficit, including Myanmar's frequent closure of the border at Tachilek as well as its lack of a clear border trade policy. The head of the Chiang Saen Customs, Patcharadit Sinsawasdi, asserted that the Thai trade deficit with Myanmar was "due to stiff and unfair Burmese trade barriers" as well as "a loss of market share to China and Singapore."[26] Another Thai Customs Department official anonymously proposed that Thailand and Myanmar engage in talks to eradicate Myanmar's "protectionism." At the same time, Mr. Sinsawasdi offered that, as a way to reduce the trade deficit, Thailand should increasingly use Myanmar as a transit point to export Thai products to China, India, and Bangladesh.[27]

Ethnic Chinese Business Networks

Ethnic Chinese businesspeople have played an important role in bolstering cross-border commerce across the Golden Triangle. Chen Xiangming highlights this fact, stressing that ethnic Chinese in the Mekong subregion have been essential entrepreneurial actors all along the frontier, given their ethnic, linguistic, and kinship networks with each other and with mainland Chinese.[28]

Indeed, the ethnic Chinese control a major part of the Mae Sai-Tachilek frontier commerce. This includes trading in gold and currency (the yuan and the baht). Currency trading is authorized by the Thai government and helps attract mainland Chinese tourists since they can bring in yuan directly from China. Tourists from China, Taiwan, and Japan constitute the majority of clients for gold. The Chinese business sector is significantly reduced whenever the border is closed.

Most consumer products sold at Mae Sai are actually imported from the eastern coastal industrial zones of China, especially in Guangdong Province. These cheap and affordable products, including clothes, shoes, and other commodities, arrive by truck from Bangkok. The Sino-Thai border trade is concentrated in Mae Sai as well as Chiang Saen. Due to the many restrictions to land routes in Myanmar, however, the bulk of these imports from China now arrives in Thailand mainly via the Mekong River since the Chinese prefer to use Chiang Saen as their entrepot.

Yunnan Province has invested RMB5 billion in building an SEZ in Chiang Saen (see chapter 7). This should boost the overall value of border trade in northern Thailand in future. Since 2006, a steadily increasing number of tourists have also been arriving from China via the Mekong River.[29]

The View on the Ground

Despite the optimistic forecasts and plans for NSEC R3B, the present study (via extended interviewing of both Thai and Myanmar merchants) reveals that Mae Sai-Tachilek border trade is increasing in a somewhat lukewarm manner along with the economic growth of these towns themselves. Stiff barriers remain. Tariffs are higher in Tachilek than in Mae Sai even for permitted commodities. Also, from Tachilek to Myanmar's interior, there are as many as 300 "unofficial checkpoints" where merchants must pay toll fees! Border merchants in Tachilek often mix taxable legal and black market goods together to reduce consumer prices. Indeed, many imitation goods are readily available. For businesspeople and transport operators, the growing ease in the logistics of cross-border trade may be offset by the high number of bribes and tolls they have to pay.[30]

Motor vehicle spare parts are a case in point. Myanmar cannot produce the parts that it needs while importing them legally is difficult. Traders have to pay a "logistics" fee of about ThB30 for each item and another fee of about ThB150 from Mae Sai to Tachilek. Merchants circumvent the restrictions by smuggling the spare parts in the bottom of trucks and placing legal goods in the upper compartment. As a result, such motor vehicle spare part prices in Myanmar are 30 percent higher than in Thailand.

Nevertheless, Thai businesses continue to export an increasing amount of goods to Myanmar. For example, ten petroleum bowsers (tanker trucks) per day go into Myanmar from Thailand. Construction materials are also exported from Thailand to Myanmar at a rate of about sixty trucks daily. Thailand's principal import from Myanmar via Mae Sai is teakwood from the Salween River region.[31]

Goods are transported by truck over the new bridge. On the old bridge, which is now mostly used as a pedestrian crossing (including by tourists), goods are also hand-carried by porters who are day workers from Myanmar. Bicycles or small pushcarts are also used on the old bridge but freight vehicles are no longer allowed; they have to use the new bridge.

One merchant informed us that his company transports goods that are ordered in Mandalay and Yangon in Myanmar. Bangkok office staff will procure the goods to fulfill the order and these are then transported from Bangkok to Chiang Rai and Mae Sai. There, the goods are repacked before being transported by truck across the new bridge from Mae Sai into Tachilek.[32]

Among the border points of Mae Sai-Tachilek, Mae Sot-Myawaddy, and Ranong-Kawthaung, the first two (both being land crossings) are preferred, in terms of lower cost, risk, and wastage. However, intermittent battles between ethnic rebel armies and the government forces (Tatmadaw) render one of the crossings inaccessible or to be avoided from time to time.[33]

The value of border trade between Mae Sai and Tachilek is estimated by local businesspeople to be about ThB20 million a day from the Thai side alone. In mid-2008, some border merchants lamented that business was not as good as in previous years. Others see trade between China and Thailand expanding significantly in the future, however, although it will occur mostly through Chiang Saen port and Chiang Khong rather than Mae Sai.

At present, Myanmar continues to enjoy a large trade volume with northern Thailand. With the completion of the NSEC road through

Gate into Tachilek, Myanmar

Myanmar, increasing numbers of Chinese tourists are coming to Mae Sai but there has been no increase in the volume of cargo. According to these informants, overland border trade between Myanmar and China largely takes place at another Myanmar border town, Shweli.[34]

These merchants also tend to believe that Thailand's 2006 military coup has had little effect on the Mae Sai-Tachilek border trade. Business is about the same as it was before the coup. Border trade here is also seasonal. During the rainy season, it is low and then in the cool or dry seasons the trade volume increases significantly. One merchant estimates that this would increase in value to ThB60 million a day when the entire GMS network of highways is completed.[35]

As for types of products coming through Tachilek to Mae Sai, they are mainly durable goods; the majority of these tend to be Chinese products in transit. Most of the goods arriving from Kengtung, to Tachilek and then to Mae Sai, are snacks, clothes, and gems—rubies and jade. Goods from India are mainly ingredients for betel-chewing. Roughly 50 percent of the goods moving between Mae Sai and Tachilek are from China, 40 percent are from Thailand, and the remaining 10 percent from Myanmar.

The lack of systematized (or computerized) customs records has significantly hindered Mae Sai-Tachilek border trade. Every month the Tachilek border officials ask their Mae Sai counterparts for a copy of their records because of their own weak record-keeping infrastructure. Moreover, "trade payments in Myanmar must be made in cash as Myanmar banks have invariably not been dependable."[36] With such constraints, traders generally have to expend more time and money on the Myanmar side of the border. In addition, Myanmar keeps a rather elusive list of forbidden imports, such as the ubiquitous flavor-enhancing ingredient, Ajinomoto (monosodium glutamate). Furthermore, Myanmar's taxes are rather opaque and arbitrary in comparison with those of Thailand.

Finally, the merchants affirm that the main competition is with the river. The Joint Committee on Coordination of Commercial Navigation (JCCCN) of the four upstream Mekong countries (China, Laos,

Myanmar and Thailand) has been addressing the issues of transportation of liquefied petroleum gas (LPG) and petroleum products, including matters relating to port taxes on both. The transportation of these fuels underlines the Mekong's growing trade significance. Myanmar in particular, though it exports some crude petroleum products and LPG,[37] has been highly dependent on energy imports especially refined petroleum, largely from Thailand and China, since 1990.[38]

In terms of transit taxes, Myanmar will benefit from the role of its border port of Wan Pon at Tachilek. The Wan Pon port checkpoint in Myanmar was upgraded on January 29, 2007 along with the Ban Muang Mom checkpoint in Laos, to meet international standards and boost arrivals of international tourists.[39] According to a customs official in Mae Sai, an increasing percentage of products from China (as much as 50 percent) may pass through Wan Pon rather than Tachilek, which could seriously affect the Tachilek-Mae Sai economy.[40]

In 2008, there was as yet little competition for R3B from R3A through Laos; the construction of the bridge at Chiang Khong-Houayxay is likely to change this, however. Moreover, Chiang Saen as a whole continues to overshadow Mae Sai as an entrepot since it allows for both river and road connections. Still, Mae Sai's economy almost totally revolves around the border trade[41] and the town continues to be a key node for frontier commerce between northern Thailand and Myanmar.

Casino Tourism

While the border trade volume and revenue fluctuates in Tachilek, the town is increasingly turning to tourism, especially casino tourism. The city boasts no less than three legal casino-hotels—Regina Hotel & Gold Club, Allure Resort, and the Mekong River Hotel (referred to as the Nine-Story Hotel)—each open twenty-four hours a day to all but Myanmar nationals. Each hotel attracts large numbers of Thai and Chinese gamblers daily. The Regina, which opened in 2001, has fifty gaming machines, fifty hotel rooms, a golf course, and a restaurant. It earns approximately ThB10 million daily.[42] Meanwhile, the Allure, inaugurated in 2003, boasts a hundred and thirty-three gaming machines, sixteen table games, ninety hotel rooms, and a restaurant. Finally, the much smaller Mekong Hotel has only six baccarat tables. Each hotel is fully owned by Thai investors on thirty-year concessions and the majority of the senior staff at these hotels is Thai.[43]

Political connections have helped the casinos prosper. For example, Regina Hotel is owned by Kiatichai Chaichaowarat, an ex-member of Thailand's Lower House from Udon Thani Province.[44] Chaichaowarat's group is able to operate thanks to its harmonious ties with authorities on both sides of the border.

Across the border in Mae Sai, more hotels have been built to house growing numbers of mostly Thai tourists, who would prefer to stay in Thailand while visiting the Myanmar casino. This habit has been facilitated by easy-to-obtain and cheap all-day border passes between Mae Sai and Tachilek; the cost of crossing the border for ASEAN nationals is ThB50, whereas for non-ASEAN nationals, it is ThB500.

Ultimately, border trade and frontier tourism have continued to accelerate at the Mae Sai-Tachilek boundary crossing point. With the widening of R3B, the maintenance of good relations between Yangon and Bangkok, and the Myanmar government's continuing ability to maintain order on the Tachilek side, cross-border prosperity will most likely prevail.

4

From Mae Sai to Mongla:
Ramifications of R3B

The major forms of income in Shan State, the hinterland of Tachilek traversed by R3B, are the timber trade, mining, dams (sale of hydropower), road use fees (tolls), casino tourism, as well as an underground economy —trafficking in people, wildlife, and narcotics. Both China and Thailand have invested heavily in various Shan State projects. Bangkok's interests are mostly in southern Shan State, focusing on casino-related tourism at Tachilek, logging, and hydropower projects.

R3B faces significant obstacles as a logistics thoroughfare for the expanding northern trade. Apart from the bottlenecks caused by customs and extra-legal tollbooths, the two-lane highway is already in need of repair as well as expansion, and it is difficult to obtain vehicles that can go the distance from Tachilek to Mongla.[1] In addition, while R3B passes through the various Special Regions created after negotiated ceasefires with the various ethnic armies, intermittent skirmishes between the Myanmar and ethnic armies still cause delays or closures at Tachilek.

From Tachilek to Mongla

The 275 kilometer long R3B begins at Tachilek, passes through Mongphyak, and leads to Kengtung—a total of 163 kilometers. Kengtung (Kyaingtong) is a historic center for the Khun culture as well as a myriad other cultures (including Shan, Wa, Lahu, and Akha). The city is built around a scenic lake and has the potential to develop a thriving tourism industry. Some locals say that Thailand's tourism boom in 2005 and 2006 had a ripple effect that benefited Kengtung.

Unfortunately, Kengtung does not enjoy a reliable electricity supply and the local authorities seem to be unwilling or unable to improve the city's infrastructure as well as promote its attractions, hence tourism-led development remains a long way off. The town does have an airport, however. Kengtung is also a way-station for vehicles traveling from Mongla to Yangon or Mongla to Tachilek along R3B.[2]

R3B from Mae Sai to Mongla

The Story of R3B: From Battles to Road Concessions

From Kengtung, R3B meanders 92 kilometers northward to Mongma until (just 10 kilometers ahead) it reaches Mongla on the Chinese border. Just across the border is Daluo. The completion of R3B represents the triumph of the Myanmar army's negotiated ceasefires with various armed ethnic organizations in the region. Indeed, the Myanmar government granted concessions to these groups to build various stretches of R3B and other connecting roads, as well as allows them to impose tolls on the through traffic along the sections they have built.

Two prominent companies, representing the strongest ethnic armies, the United Wa State Army (UWSA) and National Democratic Alliance Army (NDAA), dominate road construction in Shan State today. Wa financier Wei Hsueh Kang's Hong Pang Company has constructed roads north from Tachilek, while Lin Mingxian's Green Light and Asia Wealth companies are busy in the east. Both Wei and Lin cleverly use profits from various sources to construct roads and in turn generate income from their own "toll fees." These companies collect a tax of ThB20 per bicycle, ThB50 per motorbike, ThB200 per van, and ThB500 per truck using the roads. They also collect taxes for transported goods by weight.[3]

The entire network of NSEC roads through the Shan State has been constructed by two sources:[4]

- Tachilek–Kengtung road (163 kilometers) by UWSA's Hong Pang Company, led by Bao Youxiang. It was completed in 2004;
- Kengtung–Mongla road (90 kilometers) by NDAA's Asia Wealth Company, led by Lin Mingxian (alias Sai Lin). It was completed in 2000;
- Mongphyak–Mongyawng by Lin Mingxian's Green Light Company;
- Kengtung–Monghkok road by Hong Pang Company (Wei Hsueh Kang);
- Kengtung–Mongyawng road by Hong Pang Company;
- Taunggyi–Meiktila road by Asia World Company (Law Hsing Han and son Steven Law);
- Lashio–Nawngkhio road by Asia World Company; and
- Lashio–Muse road by Asia World Company.

Asia Wealth and Green Light are part of Sai Lin's business empire, centered in Mongla. It is Lin who developed the frontier outposts of Eu Si Lin, Mongla, Mongma, and Sop Lwe in Shan State. Since he runs Special Region Number Four (following his 1989 agreement with the Myanmar government), Sai Lin has been able to lease out almost all of Mongla's real estate to Chinese investors.[5] Indeed, Chinese capital has financed modern Mongla. Mongla operates as a fully Chinese enclave. Chinese is thus the language spoken in Mongla and the yuan is the de facto currency. Established by Sai Lin around 1994, Mongla became a Chinese casino-tourist town with close to twenty flights per day to and from the city of Daluo (on the Chinese side of the border). Chinese clientele swarmed across the frontier to gamble in Mongla's casinos. As in Tachilek, casinos have contributed to making Mongla's economy quite robust.

Three principal gaming houses originally formed the backbone of Mongla's casino economy. In January 2005, however, Chinese troops, responding to growing gang-related violence in Mongla, crossed the border into Myanmar, raiding the casinos and arresting over sixty Chinese clients.[6] The Chinese then pressured Lin to move his casinos to Wan Sieo, Mongma, 16 kilometers from the Chinese border. When the Chinese threatened to cut Mongla's electricity, Sai Lin had a power plant built in 2005, which generates enough to supply the whole town. However, Mongla's telecommunications infrastructure continues to be controlled by China and the city is almost entirely reliant on Chinese imports as well as investments.[7]

Region Four's casino gaming continues on in Mongma, where there are at least ten gaming houses. Meanwhile, Lin has been moving his investments to Boten, Laos, on the other NSEC route, R3A, where he has established a new casino (see chapter 6). Lin's Mongma casinos are simultaneously serving as a training station "for youths coming from Laos to learn the trade."[8]

Mongma is a tiny pit-stop of a town, containing only casinos and noodle-shops, all looking as if they had just been built. Beyond Mongma, the road continues through newly constructed villages containing some of the people who were evicted from the new Mongma to make way for the casinos. On either side of the roads are Chinese-owned mango and rubber plantations. The Chinese are also investing in Mongla's tobacco and sugar estates.

Mongla is a modern-looking, medium-sized town with a number of hotels, souvenir shops, discotheques, karaoke bars, brothels, and pubs. The La River, meandering through town, is crossed by a couple of elegant bridges. In the early morning, caged wild animals (some endangered) go on sale. Some of the market's customers are on the hunt for exotic meats. In addition to selling wild animals, many Akha in the

Tourist map of the "Bustling Border Town of Mongla." The map, in Chinese and Burmese, is from a brochure that the authors acquired from Sai Lin's Shwe Linn Star Tourism Company in Mongla. The border with China to the east of the La River is depicted on the right-hand side of the map.

vicinity come to Mongla to sell fresh vegetables and mountain herbs. Chinese merchants in Mongla sell vegetables, fresh flowers, food, clothes, cell phones, CDs, DVDs, and cigarettes.[9]

Mongla has an extremely large red-light district. Both boys and girls (some of whom are younger than fifteen) engage in this commercial sex work. Most of the commercial sex or massage workers in Mongla come from the border area of Yunnan Province in China and Myanmar. The majority are thus ethnic Chinese though there are some who are Akha and Shan. All in all, there are about 200 massage workers and 30 massage establishments around Mongla, including massage service centers at hotels and massage salons along the streets. Due to Mongla's shrinking tourist economy (after the shifting of the casinos to Mongma), the massage business seems to have become more difficult in 2007 and 2008.[10]

Gamblers must now drive to Mongma for roulette, blackjack, baccarat, slot machines, or other games. Many hotels in Mongla have a free shuttle service between Mongla and Mongma, however. But Mongla's economy increasingly relies on frontier commerce. The border trade between Mongla and Daluo appears to be growing, driven by China's need for industrial inputs as well as markets. There may have been as much as a 50 percent growth in cross-border trade between 2007 and 2008.[11] The diminishing of casino tourism and the rise of border trade is changing the character of Mongla's economy.

Mongla today looks like yesterday's playground. Though tourism still exists and hotels and entertainment venues abound, they are now much emptier than they once were. Empty parking lots dot the old gaming town. Sai Lin also monopolizes tourism in Mongla through his Shwe Lin Star Tourism Company. Shwe Lin manages the tourist attractions in and around Mongla, including tours to ethnic minority villages, nature sites (such as waterfalls), and a pagoda close to Myanmar's boundary with China at Mongla that contains a *tazaung*—a large pavilion bearing an inscription in Burmese that it was donated by the Chief of Special Region Number Four, U Sai Lin, and his family.

Last but not least, Mongla has a Narcotics Eradication Museum (built in 1997), which trumpets the accomplishments of Sai Lin's

The entrance to the temple in Mongla donated by the chief of Special Region Number Four, U Sai Lin, and family

Region Four in apparently eradicating opium-growing in the area. While no opium appears to be growing in the immediate vicinity of Mongla (at least along the roads) there has been an resurgence in its cultivation, however.[12]

Tolls and Potholes

Route R3B is still a two-lane thoroughfare (narrower than the Thai equivalent) and although it is slowly being enlarged from Tachilek to Kengtung, the quality needs to be improved. When this widening is completed and there is also perhaps a regional free-trade zone, the value of trade may double or triple from the current ThB20 million to ThB60 million.[13] The road transport cost per trip in Myanmar from Kengtung to Tachilek is about kyat 1,500 or ThB40.00 (equivalent market rate of kyat 38.00 = ThB1.00 in 2008).

Everyday, about forty to fifty freight vehicles make the journey from Mongla to Kengtung (or Kengtung to Mongla).[14] Approximately thirty to forty such vehicles travel daily between Kengtung and Tachilek.[15] R3B's Tachilek–Kengtung segment itself has four official "toll" checkpoints, at Mak Yang, Ta Lay, Monghpayak, and Kengtung. Each checkpoint has two toll gates where road users have to pay fees: a government gate and a gate operated by the private companies. There are also five "no pay" tollbooths (only requiring paperwork) interspersed amidst the four official stations. These multiple checkpoints and tolls are certainly not making trade across R3B any faster or more efficient and the purported one-stop service is meaningless.

As for travel time across R3B, it used to take nine to ten hours merely from Tachilek to Kengtung. But since R3B was completed and paved, the time from Tachilek to Kengtung has been reduced to four hours while the entire Tachilek–Mongla journey is six hours. This is two hours longer than travel time along R3A through Laos because: the route is longer (275 kilometers through Myanmar compared to 263 kilometers through Laos); the multiple toll gates along R3B; and the poor road quality in certain areas.

Section of R3B being resurfaced, June 2008

Indeed, the first 10 kilometers of road from Kengtung to Mongla is currently so heavily potholed and uneven that it is difficult for vehicles to pass through the area. A local driver stated that the road's dismal condition is due to two related factors: the road had been constructed shabbily, with only a superficial layer of pavement; and hence, the heavy Chinese freight trucks using R3B have destroyed this weak asphalt.[16]

Table 4.1   Segments of Route R3B: Activities, Costs, Distances, Time, and Reliability

Route	Activity	Cost (US$/ton)	Distance (km)	Time (hours)	Reliability
Bangkok-Chiang Rai	Transport	28	830	10	High
Chiang Rai-Mae Sai	Transport	28	60	1	High
Mae Sai-Tachilek	Border crossing	3	Less than 1	2	Low
Tachilek-Mongla	Transport	228 (not incl. bribes)	275	10	Low
Mongla-Daluo	Border crossing	140	Less than 1	6	Low
Daluo-Kunming	Transport	57	674	8	Medium
Within Kunming	Warehouse distribution	7; 7	50	8	High
Total	n.a.	498	1.891	45	Medium

Sources: Based upon data provided by Prathan Insayong (Siam South China Logistics) and authors' personal observations along R3B.

Table 4.1 illustrates the distance and costs for different segments along the entire NSEC using R3B. Notice that the travel time from Bangkok to Chiang Rai and from Daluo to Kunming each equal the much shorter distance between Tachilek and Mongla, attesting to the increasing inadequacy of R3B as a freight transit route.

Tapping into Shan State's Economy

China and Thailand are both seeking to dominate dam projects as well as tap hydropower resources in Shan State. Recently Thailand's MDX company began investing in the 7,110 MW Tasang Dam project (estimated completion in 2022) on Myanmar's Salween River in Shan State. The MDX group's main business activity is in real estate and basic infrastructure. It focuses on industrial infrastructure to correspond with the government's electricity-generating and water-supply projects.

The Tasang Dam is one of five in Myanmar of which the Electricity Generating Authority of Thailand (EGAT) has taken a leading role. However, a Chinese state power company became interested in the dam as well. Today, the project is split three ways as follows: China (51 percent), MDX Thailand (24 percent), and the Myanmar government (25 percent). Three other dams near the Thai-Myanmar border are majority-Chinese investment projects.[17]

The thriving timber trade in Shan State has been made possible by the high demand for wood in Thailand and China. The current selling price for pinewood, for example, is ThB35,000 per ton at the Thai border, and Myanmar kyats 700,000 (about ThB25,000) at the Chinese border.[18] UWSA's Hong Pang Company dominates logging in eastern Shan State. "They have their own logging equipment, and also subcontract other local or foreign (Thai or Chinese) loggers with equipment to carry out the logging."[19]

The Shan State's timber trade with Thailand and China greatly escalated following the 1989 ceasefire agreements with the NDAA and UWSA.[20] Another factor contributing to the logging boom was the enactment of laws in Thailand and Yunnan outlawing the felling of most types of timber. Timber trade in Shan State became dominated by Chinese companies. Thai timber companies have been especially involved in extracting teak. Consequently, there has been a massive loss of forest cover since 1989, perhaps by as much as 50 percent as a result of both legal and illegal logging.

As for mining, zinc, lignite, and gold are all being extracted in Shan State. For example, in Tachilek, the UWSA inaugurated a lignite power plant in May 2000, powered from a lignite mine near Monghpayak, north of Tachilek. In 2000 the UWSA's Hong Pang Company began looking to extract gold in Tachilek.[21] Meanwhile, in Mongla and Mongma, Lin Mingxian's NDAA coal and mineral mines are operated by a Chinese partner.[22]

Wildlife and forest products in Shan State are popular amongst the Chinese. The various species and products on sale, often endangered or prohibited in Myanmar and internationally, include tortoises, bears' gallbladders, snakes, otter skins, pangolin scales, and wild orchids. The trade continues because "there exists a thriving black market network to locate and export the various items. The main dealers are Chinese businesspeople living in towns such as Tachilek and Kengtung."[23]

Bumpy Road Ahead?

In the final analysis, while R3B offers a paved overland route from Thailand's northern border to Yunnan, the lack of security and frequent tolls make this road a less attractive option for Sino-Thai trade compared with the Chiang Saen–Guanlei–Mekong river route (which is slower and perhaps more costly but safer) and the recently completed Chiang Khong–Boten road. The new NSEC road constructed to China is only slowly contributing to greater north-south trade (in terms of quantity) but this may change in the future.[24] The Myanmar government would have to greatly modify its policies in order to see significant, lasting improvements in the Mae Sai-Tachilek trade.

5

Border Trade between Laos and Thailand at Houayxay-Chiang Khong

The North-South Economic Corridor's other major artery is R3A, which in Thailand runs through Chiang Khong in Chiang Rai Province and continues across the Mekong River to Houayxay in Laos. From Houayxay, it heads to the Lao-China border at Boten. Since 1989, Chiang Khong-Houayxay has been the only official international checkpoint between Thailand and Laos. Chiang Khong offers four official crossings into Laos. These are:

- a deep-water port for ships plying to and from Luang Prabang;
- a vehicle ferry to and from Houayxay;
- a passenger ferry, mainly for tourists traveling to Laos via Houayxay; and
- a private truck ferry used by Laemthong Lignite Ltd (a Thai company) to transport lignite ore from their mine in Vieng Phoukha, Laos to central Thailand.

There is also a petroleum pipeline for oil exports from Thailand to Laos. A bridge that will connect Chiang Khong and Houayxay across the Mekong is being constructed.

Thai-Lao Border Trade

In 2004, Thailand's border trade with Laos was the second highest in terms of value, after Malaysia. The total trade value (imports plus exports) averaged ThB21 billion per year from 2001–2003, with Thailand's exports to Laos averaging ThB17 billion a year, compared with imports from Laos of approximately ThB4.3 billion per year. Thailand enjoyed a trade surplus with Laos of approximately ThB12.7 billion per year during this period.[1] By 2007, border trade value had spiraled to ThB39 billion, with Thai exports to Laos valued at nearly ThB30 billion and imports at over ThB10 billion.[2] Border commerce has accounted for approximately 90 percent of the total trade between Thailand and Laos. Though much of this trade consists of freight to and from China, it generates a significant amount of revenue for Laos in the form of transit taxes.

Hence the twin towns of Chiang Khong-Houayxay represent a major nexus of the rapidly growing Thai-Lao frontier commerce. Border trade between these areas was only a trickle in the late 1980s but there has been at least a 200 percent increase from 1988 to the present.[3] Most goods from Houayxay to Chiang Khong are transshipments from China and across Laos to Thailand and vice-versa.[4] Thai exports through Chiang Khong-Houayxay to Laos are mainly consumer products (e.g. food and beverages), construction materials, and fuel. Lao border exports to Thailand are dominated by timber and wood products, followed in importance by mineral ores (especially lignite), and truck, tractor, and road roller parts (originating in China).[5] Agricultural products and derivatives (including handicrafts, brooms, and natural paper products) are the fourth most important exports from Laos to Thailand via this crossing (see tables 5.1, 5.2, and 5.3).[6]

Table 5.1   Top Ten Imported/Exported Goods via Chiang Khong, 2006

Types/categories of Imports (Laos to Thailand)	Value (ThB)	Types/categories of Exports (Thailand to Laos)	Value (ThB)
Timber and wood products	186,014,698.58	Petroleum	193,527,044.17
Ore: lignite	150,977,500.86	Construction materials	180,763,611.12
Vehicle parts (from China)	144,485,698.00	Food and beverages	180,206498.72
Blankets, bedcovers (from China)	36,159,750.08	Vehicle parts	150,797,270.03
Agricultural products	23,806,288.17	Machine parts	16,265,051.00
Underwear (from China)	13,791,119.95	Electronics—supplies	14,244,780.00
Umbrellas (from China)	6,452,257.51	Medicines—chemicals	4,195,444.15
Shirts, cloaks (from China)	3,960,086.54	Plastics	2,582,149.83
Livestock (oxen)	2,872,000.00	Corn seed	1,830,946.40
Scarves, bath towels (China)	2,693,326.43	Medical equipment	1,736,359.28
Other/miscellaneous	146,302,411.21	Other/miscellaneous	379,309,798.27
Total	587,515,137.33	Total	1,125,458,952.97

Source: Chiang Khong Customs House 2006

Customs house earnings in Chiang Khong from 2003 to 2007 have reflected this dramatic growth in cross-border commerce. Still, from 2006 to 2007 customs fees showed a gain while income diminished in terms of excise duties (see table 5.2). This trend could reflect the changing nature of trade between Thailand and Laos from whisky, tobacco, and other such products to more nonexcisable goods as well as fees for consular services and cargo inspection.

Table 5.2 Revenue Collected through Chiang Khong Customs House, 2003–7 (ThB)

Type	Fiscal Year 2003	Fiscal Year 2004	Fiscal Year 2005	Fiscal Year 2006	Fiscal Year 2007	Variation (2006–2007)
	Income	Income	Income	Income	Income	Increase or Decrease
Excise taxes	6,026,619	6,914,834	26,865,145	26,529,914	21,949,815	-4,580,099
Customs fees	654,997	916,388	911,414	1,089,940	1,467,134	377,194
Total	6,681,616	7,831,222	27,776,559	27,619,854	23,416,949	-4,202,905

Source: Based on statistics from http://www.chiangkhongcustoms.com.

Table 5.3 Value of Imports and Exports via Chiang Khong Customs

Fiscal Year	Total Value of Imports (ThB)	Total Values of Exports (ThB)
2003	184,558,445.18	532,207,069.62
2004	270,142,859.15	533,342,069.77
2005	413,591,611.51	901,964,913.27
2006	587,515,137.33	1,125,458,952.97
2007	783,822,708.03	837,974,133.11
2008	956,703,202.71	1,316,974,730.67

Source: Chiang Khong Customs House

Border trade through Laos forms a commercial nexus of the much larger trade between Yunnan Province and southwest China and Thailand. The chairman of Chiang Rai's Chamber of Commerce, Pattana Sittisombat, projects that 300 Chinese trucks will eventually be passing through Chiang Khong-Houayxay each day, demonstrating how this area is becoming a key logistics conduit for China.[7] Currently, Thailand has leverage over bilateral trade with Laos at this crossing, since Thailand can supply Lao consumer goods, while Laos has few goods to supply or sell to Thailand. Thailand must be prepared, however, for far more competition from China when the latter has full trading status with Laos. Thailand may lose its current trade leverage with Laos if Chinese products remain cheaper than Thai ones despite the longer transport required.[8]

Border trade between Thailand and Laos was also given a boost in 2004 with the signing of a currency agreement (bilateral liquidity support) whereby the use of the Thai baht and Lao kip would be encouraged (rather than the US dollar). Thai and Lao merchants could trade in their own currencies, making border commerce much easier.[9]

Several external factors have contributed to increasing the Chiang Khong-Houayxay border trade. First, both countries have actively supported trade here, with Thailand bearing the lion's share of expenses. Second, the Thai-China FTA makes this a high priority site. Third, there is the near final delineation of a Thai-Lao border (after decades of disagreement over the postcolonial boundaries between the two nations). Fourth, there the prospect of the eventual completion of the bridge between Chiang Khong and Houayxay. Last, but perhaps most significant, are the growing interests of China as well as Chinese businesses moving into the area. There has also been a massive upsurge in Chinese tourism to Thailand with 100,000 arrivals each year.[10]

Finance, Banking, and Taxation Barriers

Lao trade and tariff regulations constitute a significant obstacle to cross-border trade expansion at Chiang Khong-Houayxay. For instance, while in Chiang Khong local bank branches provide necessary funding to Thai businesspeople, in Laos traders are still encumbered with excessive bureaucratic red tape. Since 2006, Chiang Khong businesspeople have been meeting regularly with their Houayxay counterparts to find ways to facilitate commerce but these meetings only take place once every six months. One constraint is the mismatch in their respective administrative status and hence the level of representation at such meetings: Chiang Khong is a Thai district town while Houayxay is a provincial capital.

Some Thai entrepreneurs argue that the pervasive control of the economy by the Lao government/local authority hinders Houayxay's entrepreneurs. Thailand, on the other hand, officially allows all forms of trade relations with Houayxay. One ray of hope are the less formal meetings between local entrepreneurs and bureaucrats. But these have only just started, take place sporadically, and additional talks are often "under the table."[11] Another recent hurdle is a new Lao policy on Thai border trade vehicles. Beginning November 1, 2007, Thai operators transporting goods between Thailand and Laos have been required to carry a license issued by the Lao Department of Land Transport in order to enter the country.[12]

Ever increasing and unpredictable taxes are another barrier to cross-border trade; the local governor and bureaucrats in Houayxay (Bokeo Province) utilize "CEO" policies, constantly decreeing new sets of taxes. They can assign new taxes and duties over anything, at any time. Merchants lose precious time waiting to pay changing tax rates. Taxes are the major part of Laos's trade revenue. Indeed, the Lao government shows a keen interest in cross-border commerce as a source of income, including overlap taxes (which occur whenever you purchase goods from Bokeo Province in transit to Luang Prabang) as well as taxes on goods in transit to Vientiane.

In contrast, at Chiang Khong you can import goods into Thailand, paying taxes only once. Two factors would facilitate the border trade between Chiang Khong and Houayxay: establishing either fixed tariffs or a reduction in tariffs in Laos; and Laos's agreement to liberalize Thai banking in Houayxay. Unless these issues are resolved, it may take many years for Chiang Khong-Houayxay to achieve border trade growth rates comparable even to that of Mae Sai-Tachilek.

Indeed, the red tape at Chiang Khong-Houayxay crossing differs from that at Mae Sai-Tachilek. In Mae Sai, the transactions are merchant-to-merchant (M2M) only and there are mechanisms for money transfers. Conducting business at Chiang Khong-Houayxay is more cumbersome because Thai merchants have to wait for their Lao counterparts to obtain approval from the Central Bank of Laos for financial transactions.

Also, Thai-Lao border trade regulations are not transparent. In some cases, the Lao VAT is as high as 7 percent. In addition, while Thai VAT is standardized by law, Laos assigns VAT on a case-by-case basis. This makes it hard for merchants doing business in Lao to plan and forecast the cost that is marked up or on which they are being taxed. Thai businesspeople want the Lao authorities to have transparent tax regulations. However, it must be emphasized that in informal trade at both Mae Sai-Tachilek and Chiang Khong-Houayxay, baht or US dollars are being used instead of kyat or kip.

Despite the obstacles, overall trade between Chiang Khong and Houayxay has risen significantly over the last fifteen years.[13] This border crossing could see up to 400 container trucks (or their equivalent) each day in the near future.[14] Thailand has greater advantage in terms of border trade compared with Laos: the former exports consumer, construction, and petroleum products while Laos mostly exports timber and agricultural products. The remaining Lao imports into Thailand consist mainly of Chinese products being transshipped into Chiang Khong from Yunnan Province. These include blankets, bedcovers, and some counterfeit cell phones from China. The main mode of transportation used in the China-Lao trade is via the Mekong River, with the land route a secondary option.

Indeed, it appears that Thai-Lao (Chinese) border trade will continue to expand.[15] Frontier commerce between Thailand and Laos via Houayxay-Chiang Khong amounted to ThB900 million at the beginning of 2005.[16] Border trade hovered around ThB200 million per year. By 2007 it stood at about ThB1,000 million per year.

The Chiang Khong-Houayxay Bridge

Informants view the Chiang Khong-Houayxay bridge as a key to further growth of the cross-border trade on R3A.[17] Thailand, China, and Laos have been working together to expedite Chiang Khong's infrastructural development in anticipation of this bridge. Indeed, Thailand has earmarked ThB8 billion for related GMS corridor projects such as these.[18]

Construction of the Friendship Bridge, the third to be constructed between Thailand and Laos after the first bridge between Nong Khai and Vientiane and the second bridge between Mukdahan and Savannakhet, was originally set to begin in 2009 and be completed by 2010–11 at a cost of ThB1,600 million. In January 2010, Lao state media announced, however, that construction of the bridge would commence in March, and take thirty months to be completed.[19] This delay is hardly surprising given the global recession of 2008–10.

China and Thailand will each contribute 50 percent (ThB800 million) of the cost of building the bridge and it will begin 10 kilometers from Chiang Khong and 12 kilometers from Houayxay, circumventing both towns. The aim is that this bridge, at 630 meters long and 13.7 meters wide, in conjunction with NSEC highway R3A, will help shorten the time for transporting goods between southern China and Thailand to only four or five hours by road, against three days by ship.[20] The plan is that at least 300 freight trucks as well as other vehicles (and eventually

Plan of the Houayxay to Chiang Khong bridge

a train) will be able to use the Friendship Bridge each day. At the third GMS Summit Meeting in 2008, China announced that it intended to work closely with Thailand and the ADB to expedite the building of the bridge by 2011.[21]

At present, ferries are the sole transport link between Chiang Khong and Houayxay. Although both Thailand and Laos have ferries, everyone who transports goods to Laos on Thai-owned boats is required to use Lao-registered boats on their return trip to Thailand. Thai merchants are seeking a license to build five more ferries for this crossing, but Laos is not investing in this project.

Aside from the bridge itself, Thailand possesses land (about 400 acres) called "border control facilities" that are supposed to control manpower and products at the bridge's head, but there is still no single-stop checkpoint. Thailand has, however, improved logistics links facilitate transportation between Chiang Rai and Yunnan provinces.[22]

Growing Chinese Presence

Aspects of the construction of the bridge and surrounding facilities have been making some local observers uneasy, however. Much of the concern stems from competition by Chinese businesspersons as well as the growth of Chinese-controlled businesses and zones. Around the bridge site, "most owners of land around the site are local and national politicians,"[23] some of whom have purchased large plots of land on behalf of Chinese business operators keen to build warehouses near the bridge.[24] The village headman of Don Mahawan (where the bridge is to be located on the Thai side) laments that 70 percent of locals have already sold their land to outsiders.

Simultaneously, only 5 kilometers away from the proposed bridge (to be built in Sri Donmool village), Chinese investors are drawing up plans to build a 30,000 *rai* industrial estate in Tung Sam Mon village.[25] The estate, which will act as a hub for processed agricultural products and manufacturing export goods, was originally to be built in Chiang Saen. However, amidst opposition from locals there, the project was moved

Small boats berthed at Houayxay across from Chiang Khong. Only boats of this size can make it from China because of the multiple shoals in the upper Mekong.

to Chiang Khong district, which is more strategically located near the new bridge anyway.[26]

Just a stone's throw from the upcoming bridge is yet another Chinese project, a hotel. Chie Chou International, a Yunnan-based company registered in Thailand is constructing a 300-room resort on a 60 *rai* plot on the bank of the Mekong River. The project includes an eight-storey hotel, a mini-golf course, and helicopter landing pad.[27] This Chinese-invested hotel merely exemplifies the fact that Chinese entrepreneurs have established large trading companies in Chiang Khong and are increasingly controlling trade and transportation there. Thai businesspeople in Chiang Khong have had serious problems competing with the Chinese. Indeed, this goes deeper, since Chinese merchants often marry people of Thai nationality, and purchase Thai real estate, including agricultural land; the produce is then exported back to China. This is in direct competion with the poorer Thai farmers in the area.[28]

In Chiang Khong as well as Chiang Saen, Chinese shipping dominates because Thailand cannot compete in terms of the volume of shipping.

Chinese goods in Houayxay waiting to be uploaded onto a cargo ferry to Thailand.

As the numbers of Chinese vessels grow, Thai vessels are decreasing and unable to compete with Chinese boats on the Mekong River. In the near future, Thailand's river traders may be facing even greater competition, which could lead to unemployment in Chiang Khong and neighboring areas.[29]

China has also become the main foreign economic presence in Houayxay, ahead of Japan, Thailand, and South Korea.[30] Trade and tourism are crucial to Houayxay's economy. Houayxay boasts branches of all three state-owned commercial banks—Banque pour le Commerce Exterieur Lao Public (BCEL), Lao Development Bank (LDB), and the Agriculture Promotion Bank (APB). But banking facilities in Houayxay, as in Laos generally, are not up to par with those in Chiang Khong. As mentioned earlier, Lao merchants still have to go through the Central Bank in Vientiane to withdraw money for transactions.[31]

As in Chiang Khong, Chinese merchants have been settling down and are becoming established traders and shopkeepers in Houayxay. They can afford to pay much more than their local competitors to purchase and run establishments.[32] Thao Kaenchan, a member of the

Lao Chamber of Commerce, confirms that more Chinese nationals are settling in Houayxay. Chinese businesses are swelling and they are leasing large swathes of land in Houayxay.[33] These companies have increasingly taken out ninety-year leases of land in Laos along the NSEC (from the Thai border right up to the Chinese border), and in Houayxay itself where they are constructing hotels, golf courses, and a casino.[34]

There is also a Chinese industrial estate being envisaged in Houayxay. Moreover, Chinese investors, who established a "China Market" in Houayxay ten years ago, have now moved their operations to just 2 kilometers east of Houayxay town. It is this apparently thriving second "Indochina" market that sells Chinese goods directly to Houayxay residents.[35] Meanwhile, two cell-phone shopowners in Houayxay told us that all their merchandise was Chinese, mainly from Guangzhou— the electronics center of China.[36] The owner of a Houayxay guesthouse also explained to us that most of her guests tend to be Chinese with a few from Myanmar.

The residents of Houayxay are not particularly enthusiastic about China and its growing economic influence.[37] The owner of a Beer Lao distribution company told us that while she could also distribute Chinese beer, Lao people tend not to like it very much. She added that the preferred imports are from Thailand, including oil, clothes, consumer goods, and Heineken beer.[38] Another Houayxay respondent told us that locals do not study Chinese and do not even have a school for studying the Chinese language. As such, Laotians who are interested in learning Chinese must go to Vientiane or Luang Prabang; those who do are from the wealthier bourgeoisie or elite.[39]

6

From Chiang Khong to China: Ramifications of R3A

Begun in 1994, the two-lane R3A through Laos was completed on March 31, 2008. Only ten days earlier, on March 21, the US$4 billion Chinese-funded section of R3A (from the Lao-China border town of Mohan to Kunming) was also completed. One extremely mountainous stretch of the Chinese portion necessitated the building of 430 bridges and 15 tunnels![1] The completion of the four-lane Chinese section alone halves travel time between Kunming and Bangkok, while the official opening of the entire R3A route reduces travel time between Kunming and Bangkok from a three-day land journey to "little more than a day."[2]

Linking Yunnan to Bangkok via R3A: The Vieng Phouka Lignite Mine

The genesis of R3A dates back to November 1994, when the Economic Quadrangle Joint Development Corporation (EQJDC) was granted a concession to develop the Houayxay–Boten thoroughfare as a toll road and was awarded the right to engage in logging or to cultivate the 5,600 hectares of state land adjacent to the road.[3] In fact, this project came about due to the needs of the Vieng Phouka Lignite Company Ltd (VPL).[4] As a condition for operating in Laos, VPL was required to construct R3A, hence the road from Houayxay to the border area close to China represented VPL's first project.[5] EQJDC is a joint venture between the Lao government and Thailand's U-Sa Family Ltd Partnership. Two Thai companies—Prae Chuwit and Naowarat Pattanakarn, were also contracted to build 100-kilometer-long roads on either side of the Mekong, which will be linked by the forthcoming bridge to Chiang Khong."[6]

Today, VPL's lignite finds its way into Thailand through the help of a concession held by Laemthong Lignite (a Thai company). Since the completion of R3A, Laemthong now transports and ferries one hundred truckloads of lignite per day to Chiang Khong.[7] But Thai officials admit that China's assistance was essential to completing the road, which is supposed to be widened to become a four-lane highway, a feat that may prove to be very expensive and time-consuming given the mountainous terrain.

Lignite being loaded onto trucks at the Laemthong processing center. Their destination is central Thailand.

In 1993, prior to the construction of R3A, the route from Houayxay to Mohan in China was virtually impassable. In 2006, the trip, still over mostly dirt roads, took two days.[8] The completion of R3A in March 2008 has reduced travel time to a mere four hours.[9] At the same time, greater use of highways may reduce river transport on the Mekong. On the Thai side, the highway leads from either Chiang Khong or Chiang Rai. A four-lane highway continuing on through Phayao–Phitsanulok or Chiang Mai–Tak, then on to Bangkok, is yet to completed because of recent political upheavals in Thailand.

While R3A will assuredly spur economic growth in Chiang Khong, local reactions are mixed. Some are delighted that it will improve transport links while other Chiang Khong residents believe that there will be more air pollution, traffic jams, a reduction in the quality of life, and greater social problems.[10]

Unlike R3B through Myanmar, however, this route has not suffered from any security disruptions since it opened and Chiang Khong may become an important tourist destination in itself. China wants to use R3A to transit goods through Chiang Khong to Bangkok or the port of Laem Chabang. However, both the feeder road and bridge have suffered numerous construction delays. Moreover, the portion of R3A from Chiang Rai to Chiang Khong or Chiang Saen needs to be widened to secure other improvements in order to be financially feasible. In early 2007 a project was initiated to build a four-lane highway from Chiang Rai city to Chiang Khong.[11] However, the authors, who frequently travel on this road to conduct research and survey trips, have yet to see even the beginning of this road infrastructure project. The following section describes a trip through the existing core section of R3A.

Touring Route 3A

Facing north towards China, R3A begins its 263 kilometer journey through Laos, starting at about 12 kilometers east of Houayxay. Outside of Houayxay, along the road, one sees the red stakes marking the start of the still unconstructed Lao road leading to the yet-to-be-completed Houayxay-Chiang Khong bridge.

Leaving the red stakes behind, R3A ascends into the mountains, along which lie villages comprised mostly of clusters of small thatched-roof houses on stilts; electricity is scarce here. Occasionally one sees the indigenous people (who inhabit this region) and their livestock as well as wild animals along the road. The traffic largely consists of lignite-laden trucks heading to Thailand. In the mountains, rocky outcrops have been sheared off to make way for the new road. One source states that the Chinese company that dynamited the rocky passages was permitted by the Lao government to take the rocks and minerals back to China.[12] There are pockets of deforestion along the route, although it is difficult to say whether this is from clearing or burning to make way for the road or commercial logging.

R3A eventually winds down to the Vieng Phouka lignite mine, which is about 10 kilometers outside the town of Vieng Phouka: there are lignite trucks bound for Thailand while there are other trucks plying the northern route to China. As an urban midpoint between Thailand and China, Vieng Phouka itself has the potential to grow as a truck-stop settlement.

An hour beyond Vieng Phouka, R3A comes to a turnoff for Luang Namtha (located approximately 17 kilometers off the main road). Luang Namtha is a large northern Lao city which should see potential benefits from R3A. The city possesses a new airport, an increasingly thriving ecotourism industry, rubber and tea plantations, salt beds, a cigarette factory, an industrial estate, a copper mine, as well as corn and cassava production—virtually all under Chinese control.[13]

Only 23 kilometers from the Lao-China boundary stands the small town of Nam Teuy. It is here that one begins to see a visible Chinese influence in Laos. Nam Teuy has a smattering of Chinese merchants but one sees many Chinese-language signs. At the northern entrance to Nam Teuy is a gate and guardhouse through which we had to pass. The guardhouse ostensibly checks freight trucks arriving from and departing to China—but we saw no checking of any vehicles whatsoever. Past the gate, we saw fewer and fewer signs of any sort of agriculture.

Just 2 kilometers beyond Nam Teuy, a blue warehouse/depot loomed on our left. The purpose of this center, according to its manager whom we interviewed, was to service and house Chinese freight entering or leaving Laos. Though the depot was private, the manager was Chinese and he said that the Lao government had granted his company a fifteen-year renewable lease on the land. So there it was—Chinese depot operators doing a job normally done by the nationals of the host country, ostensibly working hand in hand with Lao officials. However, we saw absolutely no Lao officials after passing through the gate at Nam Teuy.

"Old" and "New" Boten

Three kilometers beyond the depot, R3A transects "new" Boten town. This all-Lao community consists of people who, in 2006, were forced from their homes in "old" Boten, with the Lao government promising 3 million kip (about US$370) per family. But the Lao authorities did not keep this promise and the families were evicted under duress to "new" Boten anyway. The Lao government did offer money to the villagers for new homes in "new" Boten and apparently gave them subsistence farming/planting rights. But many villagers still lacked the right to plant crops more widely.[14] Apparently, the Chinese government has contributed to the construction of a local Lao school in "new" Boten.[15]

Twenty kilometers beyond "new" Boten, one sees a sign oddly announcing the provincial border of Luang Namtha (which is technically supposed to border China), as if the country of Laos itself is coming to an end. But R3A continues on through currently uncultivated land, now earmarked for real estate development by Chinese companies. It is here—merely 5 kilometers from the Chinese border—that R3A appears to reach a country separate from Laos. This is the "Boten Border Trade" Zone (BBT), implemented on January 1, 2007 between Vientiane and Yunnan Province.[16] BBT was formalized by Decree No. 182 in 2002 under Lao Prime Minister Boungnang Vorachitr. It covers an area approximately 23 kilometers by 2 kilometers, ending at Nam Teuy. BBT is promoting the following commercial activities: trading (exports, imports, transit trade, shopping arcades, etc.), production and manufacturing (domestic consumer goods/exports, handicraft production, packaging, assembling, etc.), services (transportation, representatives and branch offices of insurance companies and banks, hospitals, restaurants, hotels, etc.).

Investors in the BBT are granted numerous benefits such as exemption from profit and income taxes for the first four years of operation and then a 50 percent reduction for an agreed period; a seven-year exemption from land tax; and a 10 percent reduction in import tax.[17]

BBT development today includes a Chinese cigarette factory, commercial salt beds, and finally, the two-year-old border casino town of Boten Golden City. This is the site of the aforementioned Lao community that was forcibly moved to "new" Boten with little or no compensation, all by order of the Lao government to make way for Chinese-financed "development."[18]

By 2017, the zone, covering 23 square kilometers from the China-Lao border at Boten, plans to have duty-free supermarkets, three five-star hotels, four four-star hotels, three additional casinos, industrial estates, a golf course, and an amusement park.[19] In addition, there are to be some cultural centers and even a stock exchange.[20]

This BBT agreement has since been altered in favor of a concession for Chinese private investors. The former governor of Luang Namtha who helped negotiate this deal has since disappeared.[21] Laos ultimately granted a thrice renewable, thirty-year concession to one particularly wealthy Chinese investor who led the financing for a 1.6 billion yuan deal. In a related development, a Chinese company called Fokheng was given a part of the BBT for a giant entertainment and business complex.[22]

Boten Golden City is—pure and simple—a Chinese town. Approximately 95 percent of its inhabitants are from China. Almost the only language heard or used here is Chinese, although some laborers in the zone do speak Lao. Boten largely consists of rows of "garages" along route R3A. These garages/shopfronts consist of restaurants, clothing stores, cell-phone shops, etc. Several are empty. There are also at least two dormitories, a brothel, an entertainment plaza, and a karaoke club. On a hill, a large casino/discotheque/massage parlor was almost complete at the time of writing.

The centerpiece and earliest-implemented portion of the zone project is the Fokheng Group's three-star Royal Jinlun Hotel and attached casino. The Jinlun's young commercial director has said that his Chinese patron is one Huang Mingxian.[23] This same Mingxian family is involved in the casino industry on the Thai-Myanmar border.[24] In March 2008, casino entrepreneurs in Mongla, Myanmar, began

Looking out across Boten Golden City. On the left is the Royal Jinlin Hotel. On the right are Chinese stores and dormitories. Only Chinese is spoken and only Chinese currency is accepted in Boten.

expanding their operations into Boten under the leadership of Lin Mingxian aka Sai Lin.[25]

Lin's Jinlun Hotel boasts 271 rooms, as well as a restaurant, bar, and massage service. The cost of this hotel/casino reached 60 million yuan, a tenth of what Chinese (as well as South Koreans) are expecting to spend on the entire economic zone.[26] The casino is itself the reason why almost all tourists come to Boten. Though a few players come from Thailand, the majority of the clientele are Chinese. As in Tachilek and Mongla in Myanmar, the fact that casinos are illegal in both China and Thailand has created the demand for this gambling hall in Boten.[27]

Within the hotel's attached casino area, there are approximately ten rooms, each representing a different mini-casino, each with a different owner. Cameras are placed above the tables and the casino staff encourage customers to place their bets quickly. Players can even bet from abroad over the Internet.[28]

The Boten-Mohan border gateway is as yet the only official crossing between China and northern Laos. For Chinese, no visa has been required to enter Laos since 2007. Lao authorities (which our team never even saw) often give the border authorization in five minutes, while the customs personel "do not carry out any control."[29]

The BBT has both positives and negatives. On the one hand, it offers the possibility of some form of economic development and employment in a remote border area hitherto sparsely populated and impoverished.

It can also bring trade and tourism opportunities to Laos. But BBT's disadvantages clearly outweigh its advantages, at least for Laos.

First, at present the main beneficiaries of BBT's trade and tourism expansion would most likely be limited to the Lao state or state-backed Lao, Chinese (Yunnanese), Thai, and Myanmar businesspersons. Second, BBT could become a mere economic enclave and dependency of China, resulting in much-diminished sovereignty for Laos in this area. Third, one could say that, since BBT's implementation, the Lao in this area have merely exchanged agricultural poverty for poverty and insecurity in Boten's less than salubrious service sector. Human trafficking and commercial sex work are thriving and HIV/AIDS and other sexually transmitted diseases may be spreading from Boten into neighboring parts of Laos. Not surprisingly, there has been drug trafficking and other serious crime, including murder.[30]

Our team also saw multitudes of crates full of wild animals, obviously being trafficked through Boten. Furthermore, forests in the area are increasingly being cut down (perhaps then sold as timber) to make way for BBT's expansion, leading to deforestation and soil erosion. Finally, the creation of the Chinese BBT means the loss of Lao identity in the area, culturally, ethnically, and linguistically.

Unequal Benefits from R3A

R3A offers advantages to China, Thailand, and Laos, though these are not balanced. Advocates state that, at least overall, the road will "encourage market expansion across borders," boost investment in the region," and "allow greater opportunities in the [tourism] service sector." Yet R3A will mainly benefit businesses trading between Thailand and the southern Chinese provinces of Yunnan and Sichuan.[31]

For Beijing in particular, the route offers a paved thoroughfare to and from the landlocked province of Yunnan. As such, the road facilitates the spread of Chinese trade and tourism through Laos down to Thailand. This offers numerous potential opportunities for Chinese traders and investors, as evident already in Boten.

For Bangkok, R3A provides a means for Thai companies to more easily invest in Laos as well as Yunnan, given the increased ease of access. For example, Charoen Phokpand is expanding its contract farming along R3A, as farm areas in Thailand diminish.[32] In the near future, a bus service (taking twenty-four hours) will connect Kunming to Bangkok.[33] Ultimately, R3A benefits both China and Thailand as it links the two countries' markets together.

For Vientiane, the advantages of R3A are far fewer than for China or Thailand. Laos can collect taxes and tariffs for through commercial traffic. Although the Lao government had given a number of specific assurances regarding land acquisition and resettlement, and road charges as a condition for receiving the ADB loan, the promise of 3 million kip per evicted family was not kept. The "old" Boten residents were forcibly moved to make way for Boten Golden City to "new" Boten, and have yet to receive compensation.[34] The Lao government was supposed to levy US$20 per passenger or US$40 per vehicle, and US$10 per border crossing for lignite traffic.[35] However, there was neither a toll station nor a tollbooth and no fees collected from the users of the brand new R3A.

Chinese or Thai tourism projects in Laos may eventually trickle down to boost economic growth in Laos itself, though such development tends to be protracted and distorted. "You [do] have a huge hinterland that's pretty badly served at the moment, from Kunming down through Lao PDR and northern Thailand," says John Cooney, director of the Southeast Asia Infrastructure Division at the ADB, which financed one section of the road. "That suddenly is becoming a market."[36]

Table 6.1   Segments of Route R3A: Activities, Costs, Distances, Time, and Reliability

Route	Activity	Cost (US$/ton)	Distance (km)	Time (hours)	Reliability
Bangkok–Chiang Rai	Transport	28	830	10	High
Chiang Rai–Chiang Khong	Transport	28	110	2	High
Chiang Khong–Houayxay	Border crossing	3	Less than 1	3	Low
Houayxay–Boten	Transport	214	263	4–5	Medium
Boten–Mohan	Border crossing	142	Less than 1	6	Medium
Boten–Kunming	Transport	71	688	10	Medium
Within Kunming	Warehouse distribution	7; 7	50	8	High
Total	**n.a.**	**500**	**1,943**	**44**	**Medium–High**

Source: Based upon data provided by Prathan Inseeyong (Siam South China Logistics) and authors' experiences along R3A.

Many grave issues remain regarding the social, economic, and enviromental impact of R3A. The road, in serving as a connection between Thailand and China, deepens Laos's dependency on these countries' economies. It also impinges on Lao sovereignty, forcing the impoverished country to offer one of its chief assets: land for the road. Indeed, "Deputy Prime Minister Somsavat Lengsavad has said the [Lao] government will trade 'land for capital.'"[37] Also, R3A's March 31, 2008 completion has facilitated the luring of young people to work as prostitutes in Thailand, Vietnam, China, and beyond.

The road has facilitated a more flourishing timber trade, but this includes illegal logging as well as the trafficking of protected wildlife from these forests. Furthermore, the road accelerates the spread of diseases such as HIV/AIDS to the once-insulated peoples of northern Laos. R3A could negatively influence the local livelihoods and lifestyles of indigenous people along the road, for example, through greater access to narcotics. One ADB representative insists that GMS governments are aware of the potential problems and are taking steps to tackle these issues.[38]

R3A is already stirring up apprehension among Thais and Laotians about China. Preecha Kamolbutr, the governor of Chiang Rai Province, believes that R3A may stimulate anxiety over a "Chinese invasion" of both Thailand and Laos. "Chinese businessmen come in with their own capital, their own workers and their own construction materials," the governor said. "I fear that in the future the Lao people might feel that they've been exploited. They will feel they've been invaded."[39]

As such, although both Myanmar and Laos have benefited from the burgeoning regional trade (at least through new physical transport infrastructures and the collection of transit revenues and fees), Laos, even more than Myanmar, has become a mere way-station for China–Thailand trade along NSEC.

Comparing R3A and R3B

What are the advantages of using Route 3A through Laos as opposed to other routes? First, R3A, passing through relatively peaceful Laos, occupies a shorter distance than R3B, which runs through the less secure terrain of northern Myanmar's restive Shan State. Second, obtaining concessions from Laos, rather than with Myanmar, has been easier for the Chinese.

In terms of costs, distance, time, and reliability, R3A currently represents a better option for traders than does R3B through Myanmar (see table 6.1) Indeed, despite the greater distance and apparent cost, it is a faster route and, given its recent construction, much more reliable in terms of road quality. Corruption along R3B (multiple checkpoints and bribes) in Myanmar is also increasingly making R3A a more desirable alternative.

As for R3B, there are some concerns, however, over R3A's road-worthiness. Only just completed, there have already been some avalanches along the highway and it may need thicker pavement. Certainly, R3A will need constant maintenance (requiring greater funding) if it is to become a major trade artery and deliver returns on its investment. It may also need to be widened beyond the current dual-lane highway.

The favored option is still via the Mekong River. But river transport has its own drawbacks; it is most efficient during the rainy season, when the Mekong is able to handle larger cargo vessels. During other seasons (when the water level is lower), only smaller ships can make the journey. In the past, these vessels were forced to navigate through a multitude of shoals and rapids on the Mekong River (see chapter 7). Chiang Khong stands on the Thai side of this potentially lucrative overland route by truck or train through Laos to China.

ASEAN has also proposed an alternative to R3A through Chiang Khong, that is, an interlinking railway between China and Singapore, via Thailand and peninsular Malaysia. Among the options is a line linking Chiang Saen with the northern Prae railway station at Denchai district, which then terminates in Bangkok. A more favorable option would have the current railway extended to Chiang Rai and then continue across the Chiang Khong-Houayxay Bridge.[40] For Thailand, however, the rail option is a far more expensive and time-consuming investment than the road.

Across from Chiang Khong in Houayxay, China has already invested ThB1,800 million to initiate the construction of a railway that will eventually reach Kunming as part of NSEC. The problem is that the widths of the Chinese and Thai railway tracks are not the same and hence they cannot be connected directly together. Regardless, according to Chiang Khong's deputy mayor, Chiang Khong must have a high-speed train direct to Bangkok because China is expanding its trade coverage into Thailand rapidly.[41]

7

Chiang Saen:
River Portal Linking Thailand to China

The port of Chiang Saen on the Mekong River is perhaps the most important entrepot in Thailand's expanding northern border trade. Approximately US$50 million in Thai-Myanmar border trade passes through Chiang Saen annually.[1] This trade could expand given the 2006 agreement allowing Thailand to import 620 teak logs per year from Myanmar (through the Chiang Saen Customs House), which could potentially bring in ThB100 million in tax revenue annually.[2]

Chiang Saen has been a strategic port since the early 1800s, first for the Lanna Kingdom, and then for Siam. For a long time, the town remained in relatively rustic isolation, facilitating ships navigating the Mekong from Guanlei, Jinghong, and Simao in China down to Luang Prabang and Vientiane in Laos. Chiang Saen has long competed with Chiang Khong to dominate northern Thailand's trade with Laos. Although Chiang Khong benefits from improved infrastructure on the opposite bank of the Mekong at Houayxay, it is Chiang Saen that has steadily built up a safe, reliable, and prosperous commerce with Thailand's northern neighbors. Its importance has been recognized. In 2000, when a flood destroyed the port, the Thai government allocated ThB190 million to rebuild it.[3] This chapter examines Chiang Saen's role in the GMS and the northern Thai economy, its competitors, vulnerabilities, and new developments.

Thai-China Trade

Chiang Saen owes its preeminent status as a trade portal on the Mekong precisely because of its relative proximity to China and its traditional role as a Thai-Chinese trade crossroads. Indeed, though Thai-China border commerce takes place at Chiang Saen, Chiang Khong, and Mae Sai, roughly 70 percent of the total border trade is through Chiang Saen.[4] Approximately 2,500 cargo ships berth at Chiang Saen port annually; over 90 percent of these are from China,[5] an average of six cargo ships each day.[6] When water levels are high during the rainy season, the port handles approximately 250 ship visits per month.[7] A spokesman for Chiang Saen port elaborated:

> Most of [the predominantly Chinese] ships dock for about two or three days. The ships often line up for almost half a kilometer in length. In the high season between July to August and the year's end, one can see shipments of dried longans, the most famous [Thai] item that is exported to China. On average there are around six or seven ships per day loading these longans. For inbound cargo, in winter there will be up to fifteen ships per day carrying apples from China to Thailand. The [current] port is always congested with this traffic as there are limited docking areas available for all the ships.[8]

The principal imports from China have been fresh vegetables, fruit (mangoes, apples, Chinese pears), cattle, garlic, powder, processed milk, clothing, and processed timber while Thai exports to China include rubber products, palm oil, longans, energy drinks, vegetable oil, thread, and canned rambutans (see table 7.1).

Estimates on the volume and value of trade through the port differ. Officially, about ThB6,500 million in goods (exports and imports) pass through Chiang Saen annually. Between 2005 to 2007 around ThB67–103 million in customs and excise revenue was collected annually (see table 7.2). This is similar to the figure of ThB70 million provided by the *Bangkok Post*.[9] Imports from China through Chiang Saen more than doubled to ThB1.22 billion in 2005 from ThB592.4 million in 2003 while exports to China rose to ThB3.86 billion in 2005 from ThB3.31 billion in 2003.[10]

In 2006, trade passing through Chiang Saen was valued at ThB7.1 billion (table 7.3) while that at Mae Sai and Chiang Khong was valued at approximately ThB2 billion each.[11] Northern Thai trade with China, Myanmar, and Laos will continue to rely on Chiang Saen's Mekong artery, at least until the completion of the Chiang Khong-Houayxay bridge.[12]

Table 7.1   Top Ten Imports/Exports via Chiang Saen, 2007 (ThB millions)

No.	Types/categories of Imports (to Thailand)	Value	Types/categories of Exports (from Thailand)	Value
1	Vegetables	298.00	Smoked rubber sheets	1361.05
2	Fruit (apples)	125.70	Dried longans	1006.20
3	Indian clothing	85.68	Palm oil	560.26
4	Rubies	73.91	Cotton cloth	366.87
5	Garlic	64.39	Crepe rubber	283.49
6	Processed timber	37.87	Vegetable oil	252.65
7	Sunflower seeds	33.63	MSG	136.94
8	Manganese-related products	26.25	Rubber pieces	136.13
9	Fragrant powder	18.40	Energy drinks	120.69
10	Watermelon seeds	10.83	Diesel	85.38
	Others/Miscellaneous	232.83	Others/Miscellaneous	1348.46
	Total	1007.49	Total	5658.12

Source: Chiang Saen Customs House

Table 7.2   Revenue Collected through Chiang Saen Customs House, 2006–7 (ThB millions)

Types of Collection	Fiscal Year 2006 Income Collection	Fiscal Year 2007 Income Collection	Variation Increase or Decrease
Excise taxes	79.5	57.18	-22.32
Customs fees	0.41	1.09	0.68
Other units collected	23.87	9.14	-14.73
Total	103.78	67.41	-36.37

Source: Chiang Saen Customs House

Table 7.3 Chiang Saen Port I: Value of Imports and Exports, 2005–7 (ThB millions)

Fiscal Year	Values of Imports	Values of Exports
2005	1,277.86	5,238.65
2006	1,162.64	6,031.02
2007	1,007.49	5,658.12

Source: Chiang Saen Customs House

There was, however, a decline in revenue from both customs charges and excise fees (see table 7.2) in 2007 relative to 2006. Though this may have represented a temporary drop on a larger long-range upward trajectory, it may also have reflected Chinese uncertainty over Thailand's political stability after the November 2006 coup. A more direct reason for the drop may have been the imposition of quotas on Thai rubber imports by China as discussed below. In any case, the Chinese are not wholly dependent on Thailand as a geographical access point to the South given China's close ties with Myanmar. Meanwhile, from 2005 to 2008, the number of vehicles (units) and passengers passing through Chiang Saen has grown considerably while the number of through vehicles, through vessels, and cargo (tons) has seen only a modest rise (see table 7.4).

The Port and its Facilities

Twelve piers (eleven of which are privately owned) already operate in the Chiang Saen port area (table 7.5). The piers can accommodate twenty-seven vessels simultaneously while total port capacity stands at 536,000 tons per year.

Table 7.4 Vessels, Vehicles, Cargoes, and Passengers through Chiang Saen, 2005–8

Month	Number of Calling Vessels (Calls)a				Number of Through Vessels (Units)b				Number of Through Cargoes (Metric tons)c				Vehicles (Units)d				Passengers (Persons)			
Fiscal Year	2005	2006	2007	2008	2005	2006	2007	2008	2005	2006	2007	2008	2005	2006	2007	2008	2005	2006	2007	2008
October	206	251	243	224	809	2408	2389	2455	8370	18603	19888	21118	169	48	119	219	592	238	646	1226
November	227	241	242	234	1191	2063	2100	1657	14918	12356	20466	14488	20	11	175	169	263	359	728	697
December	210	243	291	224	1063	1646	1944	1634	12973	12409	17734	19978	47	175	190	201	636	545	526	569
January	175	142	188	197	1129	966	1325	954	13982	11135	9034	8763	33	76	264	163	332	316	224	570
February	95	148	109	146	528	915	721	574	6815	10453	6949	2709	13	28	147	136	469	552	26	562
March	215	194	105		1215	1244	483		17682	13934	3579		58	38	155		150	404	164	
April	178	118	196		902	608	1052		12198	6737	6974		12	36	96		167	249	178	
May	179	197	159		931	1325	1418		12672	13587	11894		44	187	257		161	482	221	
June	166	195	227		862	1684	1380		10099	15426	13597		85	191	196		145	264	235	
July	193	180	228		1241	1516	1665		14418	13433	17100		37	195	220		48	276	512	
August	262	257	293		2251	2424	2694		25354	22778	27844		41	242	154		168	448	386	
September	226	212	212		2041	2667	2048		17053	23117	20903		57	223	247		233	313	316	
Total	2332	2378	2493	1025	14163	19466	19219	7274	166534	173968	175962	67056	616	1450	2220	888	3364	4446	4162	3624

Notes

a 1 vessel/1 day = 1 passage

b 1 round trip of motor truck = 1 unit

c Both import and export cargo

d Used vehicles in transit

Source: Document provided to authors by Chiang Saen Customs House, March 29, 2008.

Table 7.5 Chiang Saen Port I: Current Piers and their Owners

Pier No.	Owner	Pier No.	Owner
1	Pailin Triangle Intertrade Ltd	7	Hong Srisuwan Co., Ltd
2	Tectona Ltd	8	Chaum Pol Somboon Ltd
3	M. P. Warehouse Co., Ltd	9	Chiang Saen Cargo & Services
4	*Chiang Saen 1 Port (Public Port)*	10	Chiang Saen Shipping Services
5	Ko Liam Pier	11	Kewari
6	Top Ten Fruit Ltd	12	Nopparoj

Source: Courtesy of Prathan Inseeyong, Siam South China Logistics.

A large container port was inaugurated in October 2003 and the construction of an even more advanced container port is planned. Construction of this second port, to be located seven kilometers away from Chiang Saen—on the Kok River close to where it flows into the Mekong (in the direction of Chiang Khong)—was initially scheduled to be completed in 2009 (at a cost of ThB1.5 billion) to service up to twenty-five 500-ton freighters from China daily (see fig. 7.1).[13]

Thailand is building the second port because "the first Chiang Saen port had become too small to accommodate the rapid growth of trade and transportation between Thailand and China."[14] Indeed, Chiang Saen Port 1 saw a 48 percent increase in export/import traffic in 2005. Also, the current port provides only a limited area for support facilities

Plans for Chiang Saen Port II (outlined left)

and the ramps are inconveniently positioned when the river is low during the dry season.[15] Furthermore, there are limitations to expanding the first port since it is situated in a designated historical site.[16] Thailand is trying to get this part of Chiang Saen listed as a UNESCO World Heritage site (which would limit the type of physical development in the area) and is keen to promote cultural tourism in the district.

The new port is to have state-of-the-art container and berthing facilities, and will be forty times larger than the first port. The Thai government sees the new port as essential given China's massively expanding needs for river transport: up to 1 million tons of cargo; 300,000 tons per year of petroleum products; 200,000 tons of LPG; and 1 million persons per year.[17]

But the site of the second port is ill-suited for anchoring freighter ships, according to Kesuda Sangkhakorn, a Chiang Saen businessperson who argues that it would have been better to expand the existing port than to build a second one from scratch. Moreover, the location of the new port was determined by a concession bid obtained through political connections rather than logistical considerations.[18]

Chiang Saen Port II's construction has already commenced, however. The plan anticipates a twenty-berth port, including ramps for direct loading between truck and ship. There will be three 800-square-meter warehouses, a petroleum/bunkering berth, one port administration building, another building for customs, immigration, and quarantine procedures, a building for the Marine Department's regional office (including a vessel traffic observation tower and VHF communication), a residential block consisting of twelve houses and an apartment building, and finally, a connecting road.[19]

Chiang Saen II's anticipated 2009–11 construction and completion is to occur "in conjunction with" the anticipated completion of the Chiang Khong-Houayxay bridge, ensuring that both Chiang Saen and Chiang Khong continue to evenly expand trade linkages with China.[20] Thailand's Department of Rural Roads is to build a four-lane highway linking the new port on the River Kok to Highway 1098 (already an improved commercial highway) in Mae Chan district, and then directly to Chiang Rai City.[21]

Meanwhile, the Chiang Rai Chamber of Commerce has established an information center for the quadrangle economic development zone situated in Chiang Saen. According to the Chamber's vice president, Boontham Thipprasong, the new center is for disseminating information for border investors, showcase available resources, and expand channels of trade and product distribution.[22]

Chinese Business and Thai Bureaucracy

Chiang Saen has benefited from the reduction of bureaucratic procedures through the recent adoption of the one-stop service, which has expedited the processing time for necessary customs and other documents from one day to only one hour. Officials can now handle multiple vessels simultaneously at the port. "The introduction of this system has encouraged many Chinese businesspeople to trust Thai trading methods, bringing more business into Thailand and stimulating border trade in Chiang Saen."[23]

But trading with China remains a challenge for several reasons. For instance, rubber (a major Thai border export) has faced Chinese protectionism. In 2006, China slapped quotas on the import of Thai rubber although it is one of the products designated to have zero-tariff status under the Thai-China FTA's early-harvest program. China also requires import licensing for Thai traders. As a result there was a drop in rubber exports causing Chiang Saen to miss its budgeted export target of ThB8 billion for 2006 (see table 7.3).[24] Thailand could take appropriate action under the Mutual Recognition Agreement of the Thai-China FTA, which allows authorities to confer when problems arise on non-tariff barriers and other issues.

Another thorny issue has been that of Thai longans. Some Thai exporters had been allegedly mixing stale longans with high-grade longans destined for southern China through Chiang Saen. To mollify the Chinese, Thai officials in October 2007 commenced a campaign to inspect every shipment of longans destined for China. According to one official involved in the search, if Thailand were unable to rectify this problem, "China and Vietnam might no longer want to import dried longan from Thailand because they can now produce high-grade dried longan."[25]

Aside from the border trade, Chinese business interests and direct investment have been growing in Chiang Saen. An industrial estate was to be constructed, the costs of which were to be shared, at least initially, by China and Thailand. In a prime example of region-to-region cross-border cooperation, the governors of Chiang Rai and Yunnan provinces have actively promoted both this industrial estate and increased trade/investment linkages between their provinces. In 2004, after local protests, however, the industrial estate was relocated to an area a few kilometers outside of Chiang Khong.

Thailand's Port Authority has pressed Yunnan to have Chinese ships establish shipping agents in Chiang Saen to facilitate transport between the two regions.[26] Currently, all principal water transportation between Yunnan and Chiang Saen is controlled by Chinese businesses.[27] The growing size and number of mostly Chinese ships plying the waters of the Mekong between Jinghong and Chiang Saen have meant greater trade returns and expanding transportation needs. In July 2006, the first 300-ton vessel reached Chiang Saen; capable of carrying five containers when the Mekong is low and twelve containers when the river is high, the arrival of this ship was symbolic of the burgeoning Thai-Chinese trade.[28]

China's Manipulation of the Mekong

Ultimately, however, China is extremely interested in accelerating riparian trade between Yunnan Province and her downstream neighbors and there has been an increase in Chinese cargo vessels journeying downstream. In early January 2007, an agreement was reached whereby China would ship approximately 70,000 tons of refined oil annually from Thailand through the Mekong.[29] China's use of the Mekong as a major logistics channel for its commerce has been stymied by long distances, periods of low water levels, and occasional shoals. Hence, it is aiming to remove as many barriers as possible to its river shipping in various ways.

The distance from Chiang Saen to Guanlei, China is 287 kilometers while that between Chiang Saen and Jinghong is 360 kilometers. Throughout the year, the navigation channel varies between 12 and 400 meters in width. During the dry season (November–May), the channel is approximately 1.3 meters in depth, while in the rainy season (June–October), it is 10–14 meters deep.[30] Table 7.6 illustrates the distance and costs for different segments along the entire NSEC using the Mekong River from Bangkok to Chiang Saen in Thailand to Jinghong to Kunming in China. The travel time—at an estimated sixty-five hours—is longer than the alternative land routes through Myanmar and Laos, but this is compensated by the fact that the river route is far cheaper than using the roads. Table 7.7 shows the elevation and distance of various Mekong (Lancang) River ports from Chiang Saen, Thailand.

Table 7.6 Bangkok–Kunming via the Mekong River: Activities, Costs, Distances, Time, and Reliability

Route	Activity	Cost (US$/ton)	Distance (km)	Time (hours)	Reliability
Bangkok–Chiang Rai	Transport	28	830	10	High
Chiang Rai–Chiang Saen	Transport	28	110	1	High
Chiang Saen	Loading/unloading; inspection fees	3; 15	Less than 1	1	Medium
Chiang Saen–Jinghong port	Transport	42	360	30	Low
Jinghong port	Loading/unloading; inspection; VAT	2; 75; 60	Less than 1	7	Medium
Jinghong port–Kunming	Transport	45	534	8	High
Within Kunming	Warehouse Distribution	7; 7	50	8	High
Total	n.a.	**298.5**	**1,836**	**65**	**Medium–High**

Source: Based upon data provided by Prathan Inseeyong (Siam South China Logistics) and authors' experiences along R3A.

Table 7.7   Mekong (Lancang) Ports: Sea Level, and Distance from
Chiang Saen, Thailand

Port	Country	Elevation (m)	Distance (km)
Simao	China	651	429
Jinghong	China	591	344
Guanlei	China	531	263
Solei	Myanmar	460	195
Xiang Kok	Laos	423	106.5
Ban Mom	Laos	382	17
Wan Pong	Myanmar	382	16
Lancang Comercial	Thailand	379	9
Chiang Saen	Thailand	375	0
Chiang Khong	Thailand	354	67
Luang Prabang	Laos	270	374

Source: Courtesy of Prathan Inseeyong, Siam South China Logistics.

China's interventions on the Mekong to control water levels are partly geared to improving its own logistics and facilitate its trade. China has been constructing a series of dams along the Mekong River in Yunnan Province, including:

- The Jinghong hydropower project, which has an installed capacity of 1,750 MW and annual output of 7.93 TWh (terawatts/hour). It is located 5 kilometers north of Jinghong, the capital city of Xishuangbanna (Sipsongpanna) Prefecture in Yunnan Province, which is around 300 kilometers from the Thai frontier.

- The Nuozhadu hydropower project with an installed capacity of 5,850 MW (9 x 650 MW) and annual output of 23.912 TWh, is located on the Lancang (Upper Mekong) River between Simao district and Lancang county in Puer city. It is 400 kilometers from the Thai border. The project is already under construction and is set to be completed in June 2015.

- The Ganlanba hydropower project with an installed capacity of 155 MW (5 x 31 MW) and annual output of 0.87 TWh, is located 19 kilometers south of Jinghong. The project, whose main function has been designed for smoothing the discharge flows via its re-regulation reservoir, has been scheduled for completion by the year 2014.[31]

China's construction of these and thirteen other hydropower dams on the Upper Mekong/Lancang (upstream from Thailand and Laos) as well as increasingly longer dry seasons have caused a decrease in Mekong water levels, making river commerce more difficult.[32] This has caused few problems for downstream travel time, which on average takes one day and one night from Jinghong to Chiang Saen and one day from Guanlei to Chiang Saen. But traveling upstream is a different story. Cargo vessels normally take three days and two nights to travel upstream from Chiang Saen to Jinghong, a situation especially aggravated during the dry season.

The construction of dams in Yunnan Province has been siphoning water from the Mekong, slowing upstream transportation by as much as one month.[33] This condition has been worsened by the decision of Chinese authorities to release dam water only when Chinese vessels are going downstream. China has also been releasing water from its Mekong dams (without informing downstream countries) when Chinese cargo ships are navigating from Yunnan Province to downstream ports.[34]

Another concern is the length of time taken to transport goods from Thailand to southern China. China never informs Thai traders of the times at which it will withhold or release water from its upriver dams. As a result, freighter ships from Thailand to southern China can be delayed several days if the water level is low. Given the ongoing difficulties with refrigerating perishable goods on board, the delays often mean that these goods are spoiled before reaching the Chinese market. These continuing problems have forced Chiang Saen merchants to send their goods through Chiang Khong to Houayxay in the dry season, which could be avoided if China released dam water more regularly during the dry season while informing Chiang Saen merchants of the times of these releases.[35]

The intentional release of dam waters at times that only prioritize the interests of China can be taken as a reflection of its pursuit of a postclassical realist zero–sum game under the umbrella of asymmetrical regional interconnectedness. Though downstream Mekong states have sought much more positive–sum GMS regionalism (partly to ensure access to the Mekong for riparian transportation, commerce, energy, and food security needs), a growing challenge for Thailand (as well as for Laos, Cambodia, and Vietnam) continues to be obtaining China's cooperation regarding the Mekong.[36]

Still, China cannot totally conrol the riverine environment: during the wet season in late 2007, unusually heavy rain counteracted the effect of these Chinese dams to create a surge of water in the Mekong River. The high water level meant that over ten ships were anchoring at Chiang Saen port each day, an abnormality even for the rainy season and an unmanageable situation for port authorities.[37]

In related moves, China has continued to blast shoals and rapids in the Mekong to deepen the river, which has led to widespread local and regional environmental concerns. Given that China refuses to join the Mekong River Commission, it is difficult to discuss her river-use behavior in regional and international forums. The World Commission on Dams is the other forum where these matters could be considered and coordinated.[38]

Thailand's River Trade Outlook

The Mekong's occasional low water levels have also prompted Thai authorities to rethink the upcoming new port at Chiang Saen though work continues. Pattana Sittisombat, chairman of Chiang Rai's Chamber of Commerce, continues to support the second port, stating that Thailand might otherwise lose competitiveness given that Chiang Rai's overall border trade is expanding by 10–20 percent annually while the value of trade through Chiang Saen alone is around ThB6 billion each year and growing at approximately 12–15 percent annually.[39]

Chiang Saen's merchants allege that Thai-Chinese trade relations are plagued by Chinese discrimination against Thais.[40] Despite the Thai-China FTA, there are several non tariff trade barriers, such as double quality inspections, strict hygiene controls, China's demands for certificates of origin, and a 17 percent VAT on imported goods. Thailand, on the other hand, does not require that Chinese goods run such a gauntlet.[41] In addition, the processing of import licenses takes thirty days at a cost of ThB1,500 per application for products less than 500 tons. Finally, Chinese regulations can vary from province to province.[42]

Chinese businesspeople use the Thai language in trading with Thailand, while the majority of Thai traders cannot speak Chinese. As a result, Chinese are able to buy directly from wholesalers in Chiang Saen while Thais doing business in China have to go through Chinese middlemen. Beyond this, Thai businesspeople are often at a disadvantage because they trade in small volumes while the Chinese trade in much larger quantities.

Thai products have been facing stiffer competition from Chinese goods, which are generally cheaper and more plentiful. As a result of the 2003 Thai-China FTA and increased facilitation of shipping along the Mekong between southern China and Chiang Saen, larger volumes of Chinese products, especially vegetables and fruit, are literally being dumped at the Chiang Saen docks, making Thai farm produce uneconomical and hurting the livelihoods of local farmers and merchants.[43] Chiang Saen farmer Boonsong Sukpol laments, "Look at what happens today. We cannot sell our own produce because of all the Chinese vegetables that flow into our country under the name of a free-trade deal."[44] According to former Thai Senator Kraisak Choonhaven, "Thai farmers cannot compete with Chinese imports like apples, garlic and onions. They are two to three times cheaper; many farmers have been left destitute."[45]

A case in point is the influx of illegal Chinese garlic shipments into Thailand. While the 2003 agreement caps the shipments at 10,000 tons per year (Thailand annually produces 80,000 tons), Thailand's Commerce Ministry alleged that 300,000 tons were smuggled from southern China into Thailand in 2008. In May 2008, matters deteriorated to such an extent that the Samak administration ordered special military squads to patrol the border and monitor any attempted importation of Chinese garlic.[46]

Many Thai academics place the non competitiveness of Lao-Thai produce precisely at the doorstep of the 2003 Thai-China FTA. According to data from the International Trade Study Center of the University of the Thai Chamber of Commerce (ITSC-UCC), Thailand exported ThB7,031.97 million worth of vegetables to China and imported ThB1,203.4 million worth from China during the first six months of 2006. Despite this trade surplus, many Thai vegetable farmers suffered because more than 99 percent of the Thai exports were cassava and its byproducts. China imported Thai cassava to produce alternative fuel, animal feed, and other products.

An official from ITSC-UCC laments that if only fresh vegetables are considered, Thailand exported only ThB13 million worth of fresh vegetables to China against approximately ThB77 million worth of fresh vegetables from China. Hardest hit were northern Thai garlic farmers who have suffered greatly from the flood of cheap garlic from China over the past four years.[47] Even the head of Chiang Saen's customs office admits that "Thai farmers will lose to Chinese fruit and vegetables coming through Chiang Saen since they cannot compete."[48]

Still, Pattana Sittisombat remains optimistic about an eventual balance of trade between Thailand and China. "Thai and Chinese fruits substitute for each other: China exports fruit (including apples and pears) to Thailand and Thailand exports oranges to China (Thai prices are ThB16 per kilo as opposed to Chinese prices of ThB26 per kilo wholesale.)"[49] One could argue, however, that a balance of trade hardly counterbalances phenomena such as the continuing dumping of Chinese garlic into Thailand, which is undercutting Thailand's garlic growers' and undermining their livelihoods.

A final challenge for Mekong river trade is security. Pirates and narcotics traffickers have increasingly preyed on the Chiang Saen-to-Guanlei route. River shootouts have occurred as warnings to traders or attempts to extort protection money from local businesspeople. Thai customs officials in Chiang Saen have stated privately that the Chiang Saen-to-Guanlei river route will not be feasible until there is adequate security along the Mekong River.[50]

Still, despite obstacles, Chiang Saen's future as a hub for border trade between China and Thailand (and potentially Laos as well) seems

Loading and unloading Chinese freighters at Chiang Saen Port I

bright. Currently there are twelve warehouses permitted where there was only one. Indeed the fact that warehouses and both private and public piers already exist in Chiang Saen may keep merchants here from switching over to the Chiang Khong-Houayxay route to China.[51] PAT's Deputy Director-General is optimistic about Chiang Saen's future:

> Cargo moving through Chiang Saen Port has been growing steadily year by year…. Although highway networks such as route R3E [R3A]…and R3B…will play more [of a] role in this regional trade in the future, waterway transport will still be crucial as cost of cargo transport through Chiang Saen Port is still much lower than road transport. Also, there are no tollways along the water route, making the transport the most cost effective option.[52]

Lancang Commercial Port and "Kings Romans" Zone

A private competitor looms for Chiang Saen port in the guise of a recently established tax-free trading zone at Sop Ruak, the Thai village

Logs from Myanmar at Lancang Commercial Port, brought downstream by Chinese freighters and soon to be loaded onto trucks destined for central Thailand.

at the epicenter of the Golden Triangle, where the borders of Thailand, Laos, and Myanmar meet. The goal is to attract more tourists and businessmen to Chiang Saen, especially from China.[53]

A consortium of Thai businessmen (led by former politician Vatana Asavahame) calling itself Lan Chang Ltd, is currently building another commercial port on the road from Chiang Saen and the Golden Triangle (Sop Ruak village) itself. The private port will be able to simultaneously service six ships under 500 tons gross, and will be an alternative to the already overcrowded Chiang Saen port. The managing director of Lancang port is confident that China will prefer Chiang Saen as a Thai transport link over other border posts, especially since increasing fuel costs make transportation by ship more cost-effective than by road.[54]

At Sop Ruak village itself, casino tourism is contributing to economic growth. It all started in 1989 when the Myanmar government granted a concession to the (Prasit) Phothasuthon family (of Thailand's Chart Thai political party). At the same time, the Myanmar government was negotiating ceasefire agreements with Shan and Wa armies who had been fighting the regime in the vicinity of Tachilek.

Throughout the 1990s, Thai investors developed a hotel-casino in Myanmar, 2 kilometers from the Golden Triangle. The completed project, opened in 2000, was named the Golden Triangle Paradise Resort and its casino runs twenty-four hours a day. Only 2 kilometers from Paradise Resort itself, in Thailand, stands the recently constructed Hall of Opium museum. As with the Narcotics Eradication Museum in Mongla, it is ironic that while this Hall of Opium negatively documents the apparently defeated drug lords of the Golden Triangle, tourism in this region today has yet to be totally free of drugs or associations with the profits of the drug trade (while the erstwhile drug lords themselves are running casinos and much else).

The Golden Triangle Paradise Resort has a restaurant, duty-free shops, and a plethora of gaming tables devoted to baccarat, blackjack, and roulette. The hotel is now managed by Prasit's son Withawas Phothasuthorn, who, incidentally, is actively involved in Chiang Rai politics. In Thailand's 2001, 2005, and 2006 general elections, candidates connected to this casino stood for election. Thai officials have not always been keen to extol the Golden Triangle's casino tourism, however, and in 2000, Thailand's Third Army was briefly deployed in Chiang Saen to bar Thais from frequenting Paradise Resort.[55] But the Paradise Resort Hotel continues to thrive. "On weekends there may be as many as 500 guests and the turnover is not less than 10 million baht a day."[56]

More Chinese Gold in the Golden Triangle

In 2008, the State Planning and Investment Committee of Laos issued to Dok Ngew Kam Ltd a 75-year lease covering 827 hectares on the Mekong River at the Golden Triangle for the "Kings Romans of Laos ASEAN Economic & Tourism Development Zone." Dok Ngew Kam then teamed up with the Yunnan company Mumen to invest US$3 billion in the project to develop it into an economic, trade, and tourism zone.

At least US$86 million was invested to cover infrastructure costs such as electricity, a road, a dam, a school, restaurants, a casino, a hotel, a hospital, a commercial building, a 36-hole golf course, a handicraft center, an area for export processing, and an organic medicine production zone. Kings Romans will also eventually have an airport and a motor-racing stadium. From 2009 until 2016 there will be supplemental investments of approximately US$2,914 million to develop the area into an economic zone, producing silk, among other things. Kings Romans represents cooperation between ASEAN and China. It will also have a tax-free banking center and will develop ICT and computers. Ultimately, there are to be 34 zones. Zone 23 is to be a Mekong port. Zones 1–8 are for the five-star hotel and other buildings. This project is expected to earn ThB500 million annually.[57]

Another recent development by a Chinese investment group with minority partners from Thailand and Laos is a ThB10 billion agro-industrial estate in Laos directly across the Mekong River opposite Chiang Saen. The project, which primarily consists of a casino-hotel, includes a hospital, and market, will cover approximately 8,000 acres (20,000 *rai*) and is projected to open in 2010.[58] The group obtained the

Model of Lancang Port and the Kings Romans Project, Laos

actual lease from Laos in early 2008.[59] In a related development, Thailand, Laos, Myanmar, and China are working together to develop a cable car connecting the three countries at the Golden Triangle. The cable car would be centered at the Golden Triangle Paradise Resort Hotel.[60]

One wonders whether this Chinese-invested "casino-hotelization" of the Golden Triangle is simply a morph of China's development model in Boten, Laos. But the launching of casinos in the Golden Triangle reflects a phenomenon increasingly common to Thailand's frontier economy: the use of gaming as an engine for economic growth in Tachilek, Mongla, Boten, and Chiang Saen. In the words of Prasit Phothasuthon: "It will be Macau and the Cayman Islands rolled into one. I don't want to launder money. I want to launder the Golden Triangle."[61]

8

Chiang Rai Province: Northern Thailand's Gateway

Chiang Rai, Thailand's northern most province, borders Myanmar to the west and Laos to the north, while the Mekong River passes through Chiang Rai at the border ports of Chiang Saen and Chiang Khong. Chiang Rai Province was established in 1910. During the 1950s, Chiang Rai city became a hub of expatriate KMT activity. During the American-Vietnam War and related conflicts in the 1960s and 1970s, the KMT contributed to the growth of the opium and heroin trade that helped the city prosper, with the narco-business intertwined with local and international politics.[1]

Chiang Rai's mainstream economy grew as a result of the regional transformations made possible by the easing of Cold War hostilities, the growth of provincial business associations, and the evolution of democracy. Despite the downturn of 1997, expanding trade with Thailand's neighbors and skyrocketing tourism have contributed to Chiang Rai's continuing growth. Today, two related factors make Chiang Rai the key province for nothern trade: Chiang Rai city as the hub for all three major road and river border crossings, and hence its strategic position in the burgeoning and increasingly dominant Thai-China trade.

Key Logistics Center in GMS Trade

As described in the chapters on Chiang Khong and Chiang Saen, Chiang Rai today stands as the gateway for northern Thai trade with China. In 2004, the Thai-China trade through Chiang Rai skyrocketed, reaching ThB6 billion (US$153 million), an enormous increase perhaps owing to the 2003 Thai-China FTA.[2] By 2007, that figure had grown to ThB66.3 billion (US$2 billion) and the Yunnan provincial government expected a 10 percent annual growth thereafter.[3] Based on the 2007 figures as compared to the 2006 ones, the value of imports between Chiang Rai Province and Thailand's northern neighbors (Myanmar, Laos, China) has been growing (2.24 percent), while exports have fallen slightly (0.59 percent). Diminished Chiang Rai exports include agricultural products, iron, industrial goods, construction materials, and vehicles. Growing imports from China include vegetables, apples, pears, and mushrooms.[4]

In 2007, the Chiang Rai Chamber of Commerce and the Yunnan Modern Logistics Association agreed to cooperate and ensure that their respective members respect the laws of each other's countries. Amornphan Nimanant, the governor of Chiang Rai, stated that Chiang Rai Province would organize a meeting of governors and other leaders within the Economic Quadrangle to help these nations obtain more benefits through the development of roads.[5]

According to NESDB advisor Parametee, the average transportation time from Bangkok to Kunming over the past six years via the eastern route was 78 hours and the cost per ton of goods was about US$500. The western route is cheaper and faster at about US$270 per ton of goods and 45 hours. However, the eastern route transportation time should diminish with the completion of R3A and the Chiang Khong-Houayxay bridge. Finally, if river transport through Chiang Saen is used, transportation time increases to 112 hours and costs to about US$270 per ton. Goods can also be moved by a combination of road and river transport.[6]

Chiang Rai owes its economic growth to its proximity with southern China and access to R3A, R3B, and the Mekong River. Chiang Rai's business associations together with the NESDB have strongly pushed to reduce cross-border trade barriers and transport costs in order to improve efficiency. According to the NESDB, if Thailand wants to maintain its competitive advantage vis-à-vis its neighbors along the NSEC, it will need to reduce both the cost per ton of road transport as well as travel time. The NESDB sees a decrease in border fees as a necessary step.[7] Chiang Rai's business community has echoed this message while calling for a national agreement on import and export rules, a greater focus by policymakers on the R3A route, more emphasis on building up Chiang Rai as a special border province, and greater transparency and cooperation between city officials, local members of the House of Representatives, and the private sector.[8]

The principal border "spokes" (transshipment points) of Mae Sai, Chiang Saen, and Chiang Khong all transect Chiang Rai city. As such, Chiang Rai is strategically situated as a frontier gateway or transshipment center for the border trade from China, Myanmar, and Laos. Chiang Rai is also essential to Thailand's Mekong river trade: the Thai government has designated Chiang Rai as the strategic province for Mekong basin trade, via Chiang Khong and Chiang Saen.[9] In recognition of its importance, as part of its commitment to NSEC, the Thai government plans to upgrade roads across Chiang Rai Province to facilitate transportation throughout northern Thailand.

Goods passing through Chiang Rai later traverse either Chiang Mai to the west or Phayao in the east before ultimately reaching Bangkok or Laem Chabang. In 2000, Chiang Rai Province was selected to host the first border economic zone, encompassing the SEZs in Mae Sai, Chiang Saen, and Chiang Khong. Thailand's NESDB initiated a US$475.82 million twenty-year (2002–21) framework of development with 35 programs and 112 projects promoting mostly joint ventures in trade, industry, and tourism between and among Thailand and China, Laos, and Myanmar.[10] In 2008, however, despite a continuing influx of Chinese investment into Chiang Rai, the zone had yet to be fully implemented and Chiang Rai's businesspeople were pushing the Samak government to enact the proposal.[11]

In 2006, Chiang Rai's Gross Provincial Product (GPP) stood at ThB50,093. Trade in goods (especially border trade) ranked second to only agriculture in terms of Chiang Rai's 2006 production sectors (see table 8.1). The service sector—specifically tourism—ranked third. According to the Tourism Authority of Thailand, income from tourism accounted for 9 percent of the northern Gross Regional Product (GRP) in 2007. More than two-thirds of that income was from domestic Thai tourists.[12] By 2007, the population of Chiang Rai Province was 1.194 million, its GPP had reached ThB54,306 million and the GPP per capita was ThB45,467.[13] (See table A in the appendix for detailed Chiang Rai GPP from 2000 to 2007.)

Table 8.1   Chiang Rai Production Sectors in 2006

Production Sectors	Value (ThB million)	% Total
Agriculture (rice, fruit, tobacco)	15,943	31.83
(Border) trade in goods	9,396	18.76
Industry	3,264	3.98
Construction	1,910	3.81
Hotels/Restaurants	1,362	2.72
Other/Miscellaneous	18,218	38.90
GPP	50,093	
GPI	38,332	

Source: Vichai Gaenrahong, "Chiang Rai's Economic Situation 2007," Chiang Rai Provincial Trade Office, January 29, 2008, 1.

Table 8.2   Chiang Rai Province's Border Trade in 2007

	Value	Percentage	Fluctuation
Imports + exports	12,513.19	11.47	+1287.46
Imports	2507.53	9.80	+223.89
Exports	10,005.66	11.89	+1063.57
Balance of trade	7498.13	12.61	+839.68

Source: Vichai Gaenrahong, "Chiang Rai's Economic Situation 2007," Chiang Rai Provincial Trade Office, January 29, 2008, 3.

Growing Chinese Presence

Since 2003, the Chinese presence in Chiang Rai has grown tremendously, particularly in business and tourism. There are an expanding number of road and building signs in Chinese while Chinese-language karaoke is becoming a rage. Local college students are increasingly exhibiting a preference for learning Mandarin as a second language over English.

China has helped by sponsoring "Confucius" institutes in various Thai schools, where Mandarin courses are offered free of charge.[14] China has also recently spent US$1.5 million on a striking Chinese language and cultural center at Chiang Rai's Mae Fah Luang University.[15] Across the border, nine universities in Kunming offer four-year degrees on Thai language while other courses focus on Thai tourism, hospitality, and business. The growing level of Chinese direct investment has led one source to dub Chiang Rai "the mafia city of Chinese business."[16]

Meanwhile, a large Chinese industrial park (to be constructed in Chiang Khong) and other mainland business investments have made many in Chiang Rai's business community optimistic about economic growth and entrepreneurial opportunities. Tanakorn Seriburi of the Thai-Chinese Chamber of Commerce (TCCC) foresees growing joint investment in food processing as well as in the gem and jewelry business. According to him, "Chiang Rai will benefit most in terms of [Chinese] trade, investment, and tourism."[17]

This view is echoed by the Thai consul-general in Kunming who sees R3A from China to Chiang Rai Province as potentially expanding trade and tourist traffic between Thailand and China.[18] And while many people in Chiang Rai are wary of the intensifying Chinese influence,[19] perhaps "local people's fears of the Chinese are blinding them from golden opportunities in the promising economic area. This is making it easy for their foreign competitors to take advantage."[20]

But Chiang Rai's Chinese traders have had their own worries. For instance, the Thai government has still yet to implement a clear policy on the Economic Quadrangle. Also, frequent Thai political challenges (e.g. the 2006 coup and changes in government) have drastically slowed down many major projects, including the special economic zone in Chiang Rai, the second port at Chiang Saen, the Chiang Khong industrial zone, and the new railway link between Denchai and Chiang Rai. Although some parts of the infrastructure are ready, no clear rules or regulations have been established.

Meanwhile, the regulations for goods transported along Highway R3A have yet to be drafted, while Thai merchandise that crosses the Lao border is still subject to an unsatisfactorily stiff (2 percent) tariff.[21] Ultimately, different customs procedures between countries and the still unresolved issue of revenue-sharing across border links (bridges, ferries, etc.) may inhibit NSEC's potential for Chiang Rai.[22] Several of these problems derive from intra-bureaucratic wrangling, and many in Chiang Rai feel that the central government is doing nothing to help sort out these difficulties. If Thailand's bureaucracy cannot do a better job facilitating Thai trade across the Mekong basin then Thailand will increasingly lose out to Chinese businesspeople who are investing aggressively across the region.[23]

Pattana Sittisombat, chairman of Chiang Rai's Chamber of Commerce (and chair of the Quadrangle Economic Business Committee grouping of ten northern Thai chambers of commerce), argues that

> if Thai investors could make a serious investment in logistics and the supply chain, the country's logistics situation would stand a better chance of operating effectively within Indochina. And once this issue is resolved…more Thai businesses would be able to export their products into Indochina, with Chiang Rai acting as a commercial hub…I won't wait for the completion of the whole transport system. We don't have time anymore to prepare or hold another seminar—we need to do this now and…be ready before the fourth Friendship Bridge opens in 2011, linking up the R3A.[24]

To resolve the customs obstacles, Chiang Rai's Chamber of Commerce spearheaded the move (on the Thai side) to enact a one-stop inspection system for goods traveling along R3A through Laos. All GMS countries will be required to harmonize their customs procedures.[25] For example, for goods proceeding to or from China, a single inspection at the Chinese distribution center would be sufficient.[26]

Other local criticisms deal with the plan to transform Chiang Rai into a special local economic zone. Initially, the disadvantages were seen to be a relaxation of labor and environmental standards that would favor foreign investors. There were fears too that the zone might limit decentralization, returning power to the central government.[27] Finally, some also complained of the protracted implementation of the zone. Meanwhile, the service sector continues to grow in Chiang Rai. There are two major hospitals and five institutions of higher learning, including Chiang Rai Rajabhat and Mae Fah Luang universities. The Chinese-oriented Mae Fah Luang "aims to be the academic hub for the region, drawing scholars from the mountains of Yunnan, Laos and Myanmar."[28] Roads, bus services, and the international airport are being refurbished and modernized.

Local businesses are optimistic that by 2012, NSEC and all its feeder roads and related infrastructure will be complete—including a rail connection. Chiang Rai's economy is set to skyrocket, primarily due to tourism, better logistics, transport, and infrastructure, and investment in real estate. Although there is a direct correlation between Chiang Rai's economic outlook and Chinese investment, the growing power of local business associations in Chiang Rai influences public policy in the city. Decentralization has given the Chamber of Commerce more flexibility in dealing with bureaucracy, but continued cooperation is crucial to maintain growth.[29]

At present, cross-border commerce appears to be most profitable, in descending order, in Chiang Saen-China, Mae Sai-Tachilek, and Chiang Khong-Houayxay. While the Chambers of Commerce of Chiang Rai and Tachilek meet every two months, Chiang Rai-Houayxay business meetings are much less regular.

The non-standardization of customs procedures continues to be the biggest barrier to the China-Thai trade. All four countries in the Quadrangle must come to an agreement prior to the completion of the Friendship Bridge at Chiang Khong-Houayxay.[30]

Will Chiang Rai's Economy Outpace that of Chiang Mai?

A Chiang Mai businessman sees Chiang Mai (which is fast becoming an urban sprawl) losing out to Chiang Rai in terms of tourism. "Now, 70 percent of tourists briefly stop here [in Chiang Mai] and then go on to Chiang Rai."[31] Moreover, while Chiang Mai continues to trump Chiang Rai in terms of tourism stays and accommodation (including both high-quality and budget hotels), the most recent data on tourism arrivals indicates that Chiang Mai has, since 2007, suffered a downturn while Chiang Rai's tourism has continued to expand.[32] Still Chiang Rai continues to be hampered by a dearth of tourist facilities, especially accommodation for the growing number of Chinese tourists traveling to or through Chiang Rai.

9

Chiang Mai:
Thailand's Northern Core

While Chiang Rai serves as the border gateway or transshipment center to and from China via Laos or Myanmar, Chiang Mai city remains the economic core of Thailand's North. The population of Chiang Mai Province in 2008 was 1,670,317, making it the fifth most populous province behind Khonkhaen, Ubon Ratchathani, Nakhon Ratchasima (Khorat), and Bangkok. Metropolitan Chiang Mai (which includes eight districts) has a population of nearly one million (968,678).[1] Once the second largest city in Thailand (it has been overtaken in terms of population by Khorat), Chiang Mai city (a smaller unit than the metropolitan area) now ranks slightly behind Hat Yai, making it the fourth most populous city in the country though it remains the most densely inhabited city in the North. According to the census of 1990, there were 167,776 officially registered inhabitants and a projection of 186,807 people for 2010.[2]

Chiang Mai had been the capital of the Lanna Kingdom since 1296 and, following its 1899 incorporation by Siam, began acting as a northern hub of the Siamese administration. This role became more pronounced in 1922, when the Bangkok–Chiang Mai railway was completed. At the time, British, Danish, and French timber companies dominated Siam's northern economy. Chiang Mai was strategically situated between British Burma and French Laos. In 1950, at a time of heightened Cold War tensions, the United States established a consulate in Chiang Mai.

In 1962, the Thai government launched its first five-year National Economic and Social Development Plan (NESDP), which called for accelerated industrialization throughout the country. The fourth

NESDP (1977–81) stressed economic growth outside the Bangkok Metropolitan Area.[3] For Thailand's North, the hastened industrialization was spearheaded by the 1985 establishment of the Northern Region Industrial Estate (NRIE) along the Chiang Mai-Lampang Super-highway—the northern part of which (twinning the cities of Chiang Mai and Lamphun) gradually became an urban sprawl known as the Chiang Mai metropolitan area.[4] Besides industrialization and traditional agriculture, Chiang Mai's economy has benefited from four decades of a growing, state-supported service sector to which it owes its evolution into a hub for tourism, international employment, and an increasingly favorite destination for foreign retirees.[5]

Given this sectoral diversity, Chiang Mai's economy has accelerated rapidly and its Gross Provincial Product (GPP) has continued to be the highest in the northern region. In 2004, the GPP hovered around ThB98,004 million while per capita income ranked third in the region, at ThB61,776. By 2007, Chiang Mai's GPP reached ThB118,020 million, while per capita GPP was at ThB74,524.[6] Chiang Mai has the largest economy of the northern region, with wholesale and retail trade, transport, storage and communications, agriculture, manufacturing, and hotels and restaurants being the main sectors. The metropolitan area contributes the largest share (14.8 percent) of the northern region's Gross Regional Product (see table B in the appendix for GRP details from 2000 to 2007).

Chiang Mai's principal revenue sources are the service sector (ThB25,926 million or 26 percent), industry (ThB19,631 million or 20 percent), trade (ThB15,811 million or 16 percent), and agriculture (ThB14,005 million or 14 percent).[7] Growing commerce with China is boosting the importance of the trade sector. The main foreign investors in Chiang Mai are Taiwan (with 23 percent), followed in almost equal parts by Japan, the United States, and then Australia.[8] Foreign investment has primarily been in agriculture, light industry, electronics, and the service sector.[9]

According to Somchai Sirisujin of the Chiang Mai Chamber of Commerce, Chinese businesspeople and investors have begun involving themselves in Chiang Mai (and have a Chinese business association) and could eventually become dominant.[10] Ultimately, as the most populous and wealthiest city of the North, Chiang Mai is particularly well-suited for building infrastructure and harnessing Thailand's burgeoning subregional trade.

Thai historian Ratanaporn Sethakul argues that Chiang Mai city will never be eclipsed by Chiang Rai, despite the growth of the latter, because Chiang Mai has always been the historical and cultural center of the North.[11] Businessman Somchai Sirisujin agrees, asserting that Chiang Mai city will continue to be an essential city, not just for northern Thailand but for the Mekong basin as a whole. Moreover, he adds, Chiang Rai simply cannot compete with Chiang Mai in terms of infrastructure, services, and economic scale.[12] In 2004, Chiang Mai already had 136 bank branches (the highest number of branch offices in any city in the region). Meanwhile, twelve countries (including the United States, China, and Japan) have consulates in Chiang Mai.

In terms of logistics and transport, Chiang Mai marks the end of the rail line from Bangkok and a growing hub for long-haul freight, passenger vehicles, and rental cars. Chiang Mai International Airport has become the hub for air travel in the northern GMS and is the second largest airport in Thailand outside of Suvarnabhumi in Bangkok. The airport services national and international carriers, with direct flights from other Asian countries and Europe. In 2004, the value of trade through Chiang Mai International Airport was ThB7,035 million. Exports accounted for ThB5,709 million (led by processed agricultural products, wood products, and jewelry) while imports accounted for ThB1,325 million (mainly electronic parts and machinery).[13]

Chiang Mai's educational infrastructure is second to none in Thailand's North, with approximately 1,985 educational institutions, including 9 universities, 21 commercial colleges, and 8 international schools.[14] This includes the Chinese-medium Chong Fa school; there are a growing number of Chinese students enrolled in local schools while Thai parents are increasingly interested in having their children study Chinese language at Chong Fa or elsewhere.[15] As the region's premier medical center, Chiang Mai has 31 government hospitals, 14 private hospitals, 265 health centers, and 441 clinics.[16]

Furthermore, Chiang Mai offers an environment with easy access to a fairly large pool of cheap labor. Since Chiang Mai city—with opportunities for potential workers—is close to the borders of both Myanmar and Laos, there has been an influx of migrants from these countries and China. There are as well as northern indigenous peoples (including the Karen, Lahu, Hmong, Lisu, Akha, Yao, Lua, Palaung, Shan, Pao, and Tai Lue). This pool is especially "cost-effective," accessible, and hence exploitable because of the labor regulatory processes (e.g., a poor labor law protection); intricate citizenship requirements (e.g., preventing countless indigenous people from attaining Thai citizenship); a Thai forestry policy that has affected the traditional subsistence livelihoods of upland indigenous groups or forced them to move out of their areas in search of paid work in the urban areas; inadequate assistance from the state; and segregation from society.[17]

Chiang Mai city also possesses other attributes and services that make it economically attractive for investment or living. It has thriving and diverse restaurants, shopping areas, entertainment venues, and sports and recreation areas (including fourteen golf courses). Property, office space, and housing space are available and easy to obtain. There are many tourist attractions in the city or within easy reach. Last, but not least, with its relatively large and fairly cosmopolitan population, apart from many English speakers, the city boasts more speakers of Chinese, Japanese, and European languages, than other Thai provincial cities.

Chiang Mai's business and political leaders have continued to initiate projects to boost the local economy or improve efficiency. One public transportation project involves an improved Bus Rapid Transit system.[18] Meanwhile, Chiang Mai's Chamber of Commerce signed an MOU with the Trade Mission China-ASEAN Expo for trade association and tourism promotion with China. The chamber also participated in the GMS Summit 2005, the Kunming Fair 2005, and signed an MOU with the Chamber of Commerce of Lyon in France (2005).[19]

In 2007, the Chamber of Commerce, Chiang Mai Federation of Thai Industries, and Chiang Mai Bankers Club proposed accelerating the launch of an international convention and exhibition center, which is being built at a cost of ThB1,800,000, arguing that the center would bring in two billion baht for the local economy and boost tourist arrivals.[20] Various politicians have been struggling for control of the construction concessions and this has delayed the center's completion.[21]

It is easy to see why foreign companies have wanted to establish branches or engage in business through Chiang Mai city rather than Chiang Rai: "If you were a foreign branch businessman living in Thailand's North (and if you had a family), you'd want to live in Chiang Mai—not Chiang Rai."[22] Ultimately, Chiang Mai offers an "excellent home base in infrastructure and other things" and will increasingly serve as an essential "dock to upload products" for the Thai-China FTA.[23]

Another recent development demonstrates the confidence of foreign investors in the city. The ECC Group, a Netherlands-based retail developer, has chosen to launch the US$90 million Promenada shopping mall with a total retail space of 75,000 square meters. It will feature a street mall, offering a variety of blended brand name and local products targeting the upper-middle income market.[24] ECC has formed a partnership with VGF Design, a Chiang Mai-based company. It is to be completed in 2011, and will generate 3,000 additional jobs.[25]

The Impact of Political Decentralization in Thailand on Border Trade

To what extent do local factors influence cross-border trade? Thailand's political, administrative, and financial decentralization began to accelerate with the promulgation of the Tambon Council and Tambon Administrative Authority Act of 1994 and Constitution of 1997.[1] Decentralization somewhat paralleled four other interlinked key developments: the rise of provincial business associations as lobbyists in the late 1980s; the end of the Cold War; the rise in border trade; and the push for regionalism, especially the GMS.

Provincial business associations played a key role in pressing the Thai government to open up trade with Thailand's Mekong neighbors. First, between 1987 and 1989, the Chiang Rai Chamber of Commerce successfully lobbied the Prem and Chatchai administrations to temporarily and then permanently open border crossings at Chiang Khong and Chiang Saen.[2] Second, the end of the Cold War hostilities in 1991 allowed for the facilitation of Mekong basin trade among economies that had only recently been ideological rivals. Third, post-1991 mainland Southeast Asia saw a rise in border trade. Finally, in the wake of the greater political ease in the region, the ADB (along with other international economic institutions) began to push for market integration, specifically with its 1992 creation of the GMS. In line with the Thai government's 1994 passing of decentralization legislation, the ADB moved toward offering moral and, in some cases, financial support for various aspects of decentralization.[3]

In the 1980s, the Thai government allowed business associations to begin playing a greater role in public policy decision making (particularly in relation to the economy).[4] Meanwhile, the new international balance of power allowed the Thai state to place greater emphasis on regional trade rather than military security. Hence, the intensification of this border trade followed from the increasing promotion of the cross-border economy. Finally, the ADB's efforts in the Mekong basin depended on support from the GMS member-states. Ultimately, the Thai state's 1994 decision to intensify decentralization amidst growing regional integration at least partly derived from increased border security in the post-Cold War world.

Prior to the 1999 Decentralization Act (and the enshrinement of this reform in the 1997 and 2007 constitutions), the state (at the national level) was the only official voice regulating border trade. The central government was the traditional agent for change while provincial localities represented the principals. The Decentralization Act marked a shift in this relationship since it led to what might be termed a *transitioning of administrative rights* or *coalescing bargain*. New local authorities were now empowered to compete with the central government as an alternative or secondary agent for local development. This led to competition between the two and an ambiguity or disaggregation in terms of border trade regulation.

Increased Costs

Indeed, the greater local decision-making power in frontier commerce has been both positive and negative in all the major northern cities and towns involved: Chiang Mai, Chiang Khong, and Chiang Rai. The disaggregation of the state has quite significantly meant that not only the national government but also subdistrict administrative organizations (TAOs), city governments (*tesaban*), and even provincial administrative organizations (PAOs) participate in official border-trade regulation. For example, the TAO in Chiang Khong has taxed border traders passing through its administrative limits. While creating revenue for the TAO, this has also led to additional expenses for traders.

The former head of Chiang Mai's Chamber of Commerce states that border trade is now easier than ever before because of decentralization.

Local officials and businesspeople can tailor regulations to local conditions and needs, and obtain more revenue from the border trade.[5] In short, decentralization has been profitable for local businesspersons who can benefit from this new arrangements. In Chiang Rai, decentralization has meant that local notables such as Yongyuth Tiyapairat have obtained greater political clout. At the same time, the necessities of NSEC (passing through Chiang Rai) have meant that local entrepreneurs are able to latch on to key business deals involving investors from both Kunming and Bangkok. Thus, the push of decentralization has melded with the pull of trade necessities to enhance economic development and political power in Thailand's North.

However, according to Louis Lebel, director of Chiang Mai University's Unit for Social and Environmental Research, international agreements between Thailand and Myanmar or Thailand and Laos face inevitable local obstacles. Thus, "the provincial level of politics overrides deals made at the national level," Lebel says. Further, "Governments can make agreements promising smoother trade, lower tariffs and easier market access. But lower-level officials and competing businessmen on the ground can always find a way to obstruct or manipulate trade in his or her favor." Finally, "hitherto unknown safety regulations, provincial taxes and other such barriers work against bilateral free-trade agreements. Tariffs might be abolished but local sales taxes can nullify efforts by central governments."[6] In such an atmosphere, one-stop policies become meaningless.

In Thailand's border towns (including Chiang Khong, Chiang Saen, and Mae Sai), local politics influences border trade tremendously. Although every border policy flows from Thailand's central government, strong local leaders can indirectly influence border policy in their areas. According to Chiang Khong's deputy mayor, "We have local political influence over trade, but a limited budget from the center is a barrier here to build logistics. If we want to expand the route supporting logistics, such as linking the highway with a local road, we have to make a request to the central government. This applies to building more warehouses too."[7]

Nevertheless, Thailand's decentralization has encouraged frontier commerce on the Mae Sai side. Indeed, decentralization has influenced border trade such that an increasing number of trade disputes or issues in Mae Sai are resolved much quicker now because there is no need to seek Bangkok's approval.[8]

Chiang Rai's Chamber of Commerce seeks to look after border trade issues within its purview. Tellingly, the president of the Chamber of Commerce is a counselor to Thailand's prime minister and examines border trade issues with other chamber members, rapidly resolving issues at their annual meeting. He/she is extremely influential in managing border trade issues for Thailand.[9]

In 2003, a joint border committee was established by the local bureaucrats of Chiang Rai Province in Thailand and Bokeo Province in Laos, consisting of the heads of commerce, the port, and immigration. The governors control these and coordinate with others responsible for border trade. This committee meets every six months. If an important issue arises, a series of meetings commences and every six months a meeting alternates between the Thai and Lao offices.[10] As Thailand continues to devolve power to provincial, subdistrict, and municipal administrative organizations, tensions could grow between national-level policymakers (accustomed to vertically setting policy for the nation) and local officials (enjoying the growing windfall of decentralized policy leverage.)

Outside Thailand, local rules and fees in Tachilek and Houayxay have also created trade obstacles. In Houayxay, "excessive discretionary power given to local border authorities…especially with regard to interpretation of rules and imposition of arbitrary charges…is viewed as a serious obstacle to trade."[11]

Though national bureaucracies may officially control border trade policies, the proximity of local officials to frontier regions naturally gives them potential policy influence at least at an unofficial level, at most demanding a greater share of the border trade policymaking pie. As such, local authorities will undoubtedly continue to exert a growing influence on frontier commerce across the Golden Triangle.

11

Frontier Commerce and Sociolinguistic Challenges in Thailand

The construction of R3B across Myanmar and through Laos ostensibly means accelerated and more efficient trade between Thailand and southern China. The completion of this two-pronged NSEC land route also represents the girding of a two-tiered infrastructure of economics and transportation across the cultural, ethnic, and linguistic mosaic of Laos and Myanmar. NSEC's two ends are primate cities: Bangkok and Kunming. These ends are magnets for the cheap labor being pulled from the NSEC peripheries—the extraction of marginalized peoples.

Indeed, the culmination of this road system, especially through Laos, is likely to become an important catalyst for huge social change, leading to greater interconnectedness among the peoples of the economic quadrangle (China, Laos, Myanmar, and Thailand). At minimum, this means more linkages between Chinese and Thai businesspeople, as well as greater Chinese commercial penetration of northern Thailand. It also means that there is sure to be a greater influx of impoverished migrants looking for a better life in northern Thailand.

Labor Migration

Such labor migrants may assume the role of a potential cheap labor pool for Chiang Rai, Chiang Mai, and even Bangkok. A Lao businessman we interviewed in Houayxay says that though R3A is helping to accelerate Sino-Thai trade, tourism, and investments from Chinese, the road is already facilitating labor migration from northern Laos down to Houayxay, which will also lead to greater crime and smuggling.[1]

The principal languages along NSEC are Thai, Chinese, Burmese, and Lao. English serves as a lingua franca for the better-educated Chinese, Myanmar, and Lao while it is a compulsory part of the Thai curriculum.

Along R3A through Laos, three provinces separate Thailand from China: Bokeo, covering 6,196 square kilometers and with a population of 145,919 (17 per square kilometer); Luang Namtha, covering 9,325 square kilometers and with a population of 145,231 (16 per square kilometer); and Oudomxay, covering 15,370 square kilometers and with a population of 250,000 (10 per square kilometer).

Oudomxay has about twenty-three different non-Lao ethnic groups, the largest of which are Hmong, Akha, and Khamu. Bokeo possesses around thirty-four ethnicities, including Tai Lue and Hmong. Luang Namtha has a multiethnic population, including the Khamu, Akha, Hmong, Lahu, Yao, Lenten, and Sida.

It is the people from these provinces in northern Laos who are most affected by R3A. A recent report by the Foreign Workers' Administration of Thailand stated that the official number of transnational migrants from Laos in 2008 currently stands at 17,221, but this number is hard to verify and the actual number is probably much higher.[2]

Meanwhile, R3B in Myanmar passes only through Shan State. Shan State has an equally multiethnic population of 4.7 million people in an area of 155,800 square kilometers. Besides the Shan, there are the Wa, Intha, Danu, Taungthu, Pa-O, Lahu, Akha, Palaung, Burman, Kachin, and Lisu. Moreover, many Myanmar citizens have migrated from here to Thailand, either fleeing civil war or looking for economic opportunities. According to Amnesty International, in 2006 there were over 600,000 officially registered Myanmar migrants working in Thailand though it estimated that the true number was actually in the millions.[3]

Road construction along both R3A and R3B has correlated with transmigration into northern Thailand in three ways. First, the construction of the roads has required the relocation of populations living in the path of the roads. But these were forced evictions, with little or no compensation. Many evictees, left with little land or money, have moved to Thailand to find alternative work or a better life. Second, many rural Lao have moved closer to the roads upon their completion, since there is more access to electricity and other amenities near the roads. Some of these people also use the road to go to Thailand in search of even more amenities. Finally, one must consider the impact on migrant labor during and after the construction of R3A and R3B itself. The laborers who came to build the roads were mainly from urban areas. Once the roads were completed, they were unemployed. Some of this labor force seeped into Thailand, looking for new work. But why go to Thailand and not China? The answer is that Thailand currently has a need for labor in certain sectors of its economy; China, of course, does not. Indeed, Bangkok has recently been issuing greater numbers of temporary identity cards for migrant laborers in Thailand. (However, with the recent global recession and economic downturn in Thailand, new identity cards have been temporarily suspended and old identity cards have not been renewed. Many migrants were the first to lose employment.)

Thus, the desire of the populations along NSEC to find a better life has created a gigantic sucking-sound southward. But it is not only the dislocated or persecuted in Myanmar and Laos that are migrating— Chinese of all classes (though predominantly merchants) are heading toward mostly northern Thailand. Moreover, not all of these are cases of voluntary migration; there have of course been instances of organized "dumping" of workers as cheap laborers.

The coming rush of new peoples requires a modification in Thai policy. First, in terms of language policy, national and local authorities need to pay greater attention to having Thais learn more regional languages so that they can better communicate with their neighbours: Chinese, Lao, Myanmar, and others. Second, the needs of new migrants must be seriously addressed by Thailand's health and human services sector. Thai state agencies along with NGOs must become actively involved in assisting migrants along the border while educating Thais towards a greater understanding of these peoples. Ultimately, Thailand's Golden Triangle region, given its history as a geo-social crossroads, will become a nexus where migrants from Myanmar and Laos increasingly connect up with Thailand—economically, socially, and linguistically.

Linguistic Challenges

Will the influx of multilingual populations into Thailand mean communicative chaos? That is doubtful. One should only look at what has been called the Golden Rule: those with the gold, rule. In this case, we are talking about the Chinese followed by the Thais. Each is a prosperous gatekeeper of NSEC—though China is the colossus. Chinese and Thai will, in the long run, continue to exist as lingua francas alongside English. Indeed, China has initiated a dynamic campaign to advance Chinese language and cultural instruction in Thailand, sponsoring exchanges with several Thai universities and Chinese language courses and related activities in Thai schools. Tanakorn Seriburi, Chair of the Thai-Chinese Chamber of Commerce, is vigorously promoting the learning of Mandarin Chinese by Thais as a second language since this "will help foster closer relations" between China and Thailand.[4]

As for Thai, it will probably become an informal trade language in Laos as well as in the Shan States of Myanmar given the linguistic similarities between the Lao, Shan, and Thai languages. As such, the provinces traversed by R3A and R3B will witness a greater stress on Thai as a language of regional commerce.[5]

Burmese will also continue to exist as a regional trade language. Chiang Mai University and Naresuan University in Phitsanulok (Thailand) have Burmese language departments. The clear differences between Burmese and Chinese or Thai make it likely to remain useful for traders and businesspeople looking to use the R3B from Tachilek to Mongla.

The Lao language will most likely become more localized than Burmese, given the linguistic similarities between Thai and Lao. Still the strong Lao national identity should guarantee the continued linguistic survival of the language. But clearly, the stress on the major [trade] languages is already endangering most of the indigenous languages in Myanmar, Laos, and Thailand.

If there is in fact a direct correlation between NSEC "trade power" and language survival, what should be Thailand's language policy in terms of these distinct language speakers? After all, several of the indigenous groups in Laos (e.g. Lisu, Akha) are also in Thailand, although their languages have long been marginalized in mainstream education and life. Thai language instruction today focuses on the inculcation of central Thai. In addition, at least since 1974, English has been a required part of the university curriculum and it has long been part of high school instruction. Since 1997, English has been a compulsory foreign language subject from level 1 in primary education (six years of age).

Moreover, there are now more than a hundred international (English-medium) or bilingual secondary schools in Thailand with over thirty thousand students (half of whom are Thai). Further, more than fifty universities in Thailand are currently offering about six hundred International (English) programs across different fields.[6] In 2008, Prime Minister Samak Sundaravej proposed that Thailand become a subregional hub for learning English given the country's internationally recognized English-medium institutes and curriculum. He added that Bangkok has so far granted 5,500 scholarships for education and training to citizens of GMS countries.[7]

Meanwhile Thailand's Ministry of Education is also promoting Chinese language instruction. In 2008, the Ministry welcomed close to a thousand volunteer mainland Chinese language teachers to teach in Thailand.[8]

In the final analysis, the completion of the NSEC road, stimulating socioeconomic changes and boosting transmigration to Thailand, represents the continuing expansion of globalization in the Mekong basin. Thai language policy must adjust to these changes if Thailand hopes to remain economically competitive in the region: our recommendation is that the Thai government should build unity within this growing linguistic diversity. By this we mean that Thailand should seek to extend the teaching of central Thai to incoming migrants from Myanmar and Laos.

At the same time, the Thai government should assist these migrants to preserve their own languages (that is, Lao, Burmese, other ethnic languages). Promoting the teaching of migrant languages can build greater cooperation with the migrants given that this will demonstrate an appreciation for preserving their linguistic identity. Meanwhile, Bangkok should expand English teaching and encourage Chinese as a second language, perhaps the learning of either Chinese or English could become mandatory.

There will, of course, be challenges. Can Thailand maintain the political commitment and national consensus to achieve these goals? Are there sufficient funds and resources to implement a modified language policy? Despite these obstacles, we find that a multipronged language policy—combining the needs of globalization and localization—will be most beneficial for Thailand's people in the Mekong basin's changing equilibrium.

Conclusion

Border towns in Thailand's North are increasingly strategic nodes for commerce and growth within transnational SREZs, specifically encompassing Thailand, Laos, Myanmar, Cambodia, Vietnam, as well as China's Yunnan Province and Guangxi Zhuang Autonomous Region, though there are other such zones in the subregion.

This study concentrates on the quadrant encompassing Thailand, Laos, Myanmar, and Yunnan Province in China. Officially, this means the JEQC and NSEC. Within the northern nodes of Mae Sai-Tachilek, Chiang Khong-Houayxay, and Chiang Saen, there exist a multiplicity of relations among and within the state, market, and society. In Thailand, local business associations (e.g. the Chiang Rai Chamber of Commerce) are empowered by the state to offer input into border trade policy. To some extent, civil society groups can influence certain aspects of border policy (e.g. NGOs highlighting the diminished Mekong river water level). NSEC acts as a subregional economic zone of the larger GMS but NSEC is itself overshadowed by the major state players, China and Thailand, with Myanmar and Laos often acting as mere trade way stations. Border trade between Thailand's North and Myanmar, Laos, and China has skyrocketed since 1988. The growth of this commerce has led to economic gains for all countries involved.

Yet it must be emphasized that the benefits of this regional economic cooperation have been divided asymmetrically, with the smaller participant-actors (Myanmar, Laos) receiving a much smaller share of the pie than the larger ones (China, Thailand). Indeed, there has been a clear disproportionality of dividends for individual GMS member-states and for their marginal populations or social groups.

Laos has gained through its role as a transit point while Thailand has accrued benefits from, among other things, its capital investments and also from being the principal trade hub on one side of the NSEC. This ultimately exemplifies the fact that the GMS states, with unequal economies of scale, are achieving relative gains. As such, each must prioritize its own interests, and thus look to maximize its own returns, all under the umbrella of the GMS, which offers the most gains to each state, albeit in asymmetrical ways.[1] For example, benefits have been vastly lopsided for Chinese agro-exporters as opposed to Thai garlic growers or Thai trade conglomerates versus migrant or indigenous workers (some of whom come from villages in Thailand, Myanmar, or Laos displaced by various infrastructural developments or investment along NSEC).

For Thailand, the Golden Triangle frontier trade has been largely a bonanza, although R3A and R3B are in competition against each other. Customs duties and taxes collected have grown considerably in all three major northern Thai border towns. Chiang Saen's revenue far outstrips that of Mae Sai (R3B) and Chiang Khong (R3A) but Chiang Khong is also far ahead of Mae Sai (see table 12.1). The completion of the bridge at Chiang Khong will undoubtedly expand trade revenues at this boundary city and affect the relative trade positions of these three cities.

Table 12.1   Customs Duties Collections, Fiscal Year 2007 (ThB)

City	Chiang Saen	Mae Sai	Chiang Khong	Total
Import	1,007,477,768.98	693,620,638.28	783,822,717,43	2,484,921,124,69
Export	5,661,101,369,29	2,417,566,468.25	838,563,904.25	8,917,231,741.79

Source: Customs Department of Thailand, Ministry of Finance

All three suffer from some common obstacles to the border trade, incuding excess transit taxes (including bribes), construction delays, a dearth of infrastructure, and sheer bureaucratic inefficiency. In addition, there has yet to be a clear harmonization and implementation of cross-border trade rules and procedures (that are enforced) across Thailand, Laos, Myanmar, and China. Border trade has further been stymied by internal domestic conflicts (e.g. the 2006 coup in Thailand and sporadic battles in Shan State in Myanmar) as well as occasional squabbles between or among these countries. In addition, continued high tariffs in each country as well as varying levels of formal and informal taxes across local and national tiers, and tight export-import controls in Myanmar and Laos have contributed to the continuation and expansion of informal, underground trade.

Taxes are higher in Tachilek than in Houayxay, though there is a greater volume of trade in the former. Goods are slowed by informal checkpoints where special taxes have to be paid despite "one-stop" policy reforms. The instability of Tachilek's hinterland traversed by R3B as well as occasional border closings affect border trade volumes and revenue through Mae Sai. The overall level of infrastructure on R3B is poorer than that of the Chiang Khong-Houayxay R3A. However, the Lao government seems less eager than Myanmar to develop a cross-border trade network.

Finally, R3B is virtually in place while R3A remains incomplete without the Friendship Bridge or the new port at nearby Chiang Saen. Both trade cluster-towns involved are destined to facilitate commerce between southwestern China and Bangkok. Though the Myanmar route has had the competitive edge, the Lao route could become preferred once the Chiang Khong-Houayxay bridge is ready.

A recent Chinese study comparing the three NSEC routes concluded that policymakers need to pay greater attention to uncontrollable factors influencing accessibility, safety, risk, environmental protection, and energy cost.[2] It concludes that the Chiang Saen-Port Guanlei river route, though the slowest, is relatively safe and provides direct transportation, except during the dry season. The authors of that study find that the river route will become "the main development axis" between Thailand and China,[3] but do not comment on China's manipulation of downstream water levels, and hence navigability, along the Mekong. We would argue that, although the Chiang Saen route currently trumps all other arteries to China, the completion of the Chiang Khong-Houayxay bridge and feeder roads will eventually allow this route to outperform the other routes. Of course, this is dependent on the proper maintenance and necessary widening of R3A.

Meanwhile, northern Thailand's burgeoning border trade shows that local officials and the private sector have incrementally become more influential. The result has been a significant decentering of border trade policy. Chiang Rai and Chiang Mai provinces are demonstrating that they can perhaps solve many local border trade issues more effectively than the central government, which may be unaware of, or unsympathetic to, local needs. At the same time, decentralization has paved the way for corruption or manipulation of national regulations or budgets by local officials.

The success of this border trade has paralleled a tremendous growth in prosperity in Thailand's North, specifically in Chiang Rai, given that Mae Sai, Chiang Khong, and Chiang Saen are all within its provincial boundaries. Chiang Mai, as the capital of Thailand's northern region, is also profiting from this growing border trade-based prosperity. The Thai government is heavily financing improvements in logistics and infrastructure all along the NSEC and Thai companies are increasingly engaging in cross-border trade through Mae Sai-Tachilek, Chiang Khong-Houayxay, and Chiang Saen. On the other side of the border, China is also infusing resources into NSEC. Chinese investment and trade influence is growing in Thailand, Myanmar, and Laos.

Border commerce across Laos and Myanmar can be understood as simple truck-stop trade. Both states are ensconced within the purview of Chinese-Thai trade relations. But Thailand itself is one of many options through which China (specifically, Yunnan Province) can engage in commerce across the Mekong basin; Myanmar and Vietnam are other options. Furthermore, some respondents in Chiang Khong and Mae Sai voiced the belief that the end result of this growing commerce will be China's encroachment over Thailand's northern economy.

Undoubtedly, Thai-China trade ties are rapidly expanding through the vehicle of NSEC. But trade should be more extensive (at least for the next five years) through Chiang Saen, given the Mekong navigation pact's guarantee on the free passage of shipping and improved port facilities. Yet increasing regionalism is an ongoing process and the ensuing trade and relations are dynamic and may change rapidly.

One factor that could reduce NSEC traffic is the Dawei (Tavoy) Development Project Agreement signed between Myanmar and Thailand during prime minister Abhisit's visit to Myanmar in November 2010. The agreement included an SEZ to be built near the new deep-sea port of Dawei and the construction of a 160 kilometer road-and-rail link with Kanchanaburi in western Thailand. And this road-cum-rail link will proceed from Kanchanaburi through Bangkok to both the NSEC (R3A and R3B) to Kunming and the Southern Economic Corridor with Phnom Penh, Ho Chi Minh City, and the port of Vung Tau.[4]

In the final analysis, public policy can influence economic growth along the frontier since it can diminish domestic and transnational obstacles to border commerce. Such policies include, but are not limited to, the following: standardized cross-border customs procedures; the completion or enlargement of NSEC transport arteries through Myanmar and Laos; peace and order in the hinterlands of Tachilek; the completion of the Chiang Khong-Houayxay Friendship Bridge; and completion of the larger port at Chiang Saen.

This study ultimately reflects a postclassical realist view of border relations across the Golden Triangle. The GMS has evolved into a regional, increasingly tariff-free, market in which NSEC links the growing economic juggernaut of China with that of Thailand. But the GMS's very establishment, durability, and achievements have depended and depend on the decisions of the states comprising it (i.e. parts of China, Myanmar, Thailand, Laos, as well as Vietnam and Cambodia). The decisions of these actors to economically collaborate through the GMS represents a situation where states "trade off a degree of military preparedness if the potential net gains in economic capacity are substantial relative to the probability of security losses."[5] The Golden Triangle states in particular have utilized technology (thus expediting commerce and extraction of resources); geographic proximity (thus enabling NSEC trade and enhancing access to raw materials), as well as international economic pressure (given that gains are disproportionate;

China and Thailand tend to dominate NSEC). Aside from participation in the GMS, state dominance in the region can be seen in the state-driven Thai-China FTA, ACMECS, and JEQC, among other Mekong-basin SREZS. As can be seen from the activities of these growth polygons, postclassical realist prioritization of economic capacities as opposed to security is giving way to intensified cooperation across the GMS. Meanwhile, both opportunities and challenges exist in the remote peripheral border areas that connect southern China with northern Thailand via Myanmar and Laos.

With regard to opportunities, these linkages have led to burgeoning border trade potentially contributing to greater economic growth. But such obstacles as customs inefficiency, bureaucratic sluggishness, frontier instability, and the lack of adequate infrastructure continue to plague border trade prospects. Ultimately, where cross-national businesses depend on two bordering states for expeditious border policies, the two states also depend on such businesses to buttress economic growth along their frontiers.

Both public and private sectors (in each cross-border state) need to work effectively together to promote a stable frontier political economy. But this is a cross-border hurdle, especially where neighbors are politically unstable, overly bureaucratic, and traditionally mistrustful of each other. Indeed, examples of such challenges exist in each of our three case studies of political economy on the perimeter: Mae Sai-Tachilek, Chiang Khong-Houayxay, and even Chiang Saen-southern China. However, if these constraints and bottlenecks can be removed stage by stage—and they are likely to be steadily jettisoned, then state and nonstate actors alike will find that "cashing in" across the Golden Triangle will become a reality. Moreover, if states in the region continue to seek benefits—albeit allocated disproportionately—through economic cooperation, such "cashing in" may increasingly intensify and even become much more sustainable, thus presenting a form of regional stability in the not-too-distant future.

Appendix

A. Chiang Rai: Gross Provincial Product, 2000–7 (ThB million)

		2000	2002	2004	2005r	2006r	2007p
	Agriculture	6,692	8,828	12,506	15,507	13,272	15,448
1	Agriculture, hunting, and forestry	6,512	8,618	12,071	14,845	12,716	14,870
2	Fishing	180	210	435	662	557	578
	Non-agriculture	24,839	26,440	29,327	31,609	34,245	38,858
3	Mining and quarrying	180	248	302	325	297	373
4	Manufacturing	1,259	1,338	1,948	1,755	1,981	4,137
5	Electricity, gas, and water supply	672	623	735	749	750	757
6	Construction	1,232	1,823	1,777	1,741	1,841	2,232
7	Wholesale and retail trade; repair of motor vehicles, and motorcycles; and personal and household goods	7,870	7,893	8,394	8,891	9,197	9,503
8	Hotels and restaurants	1,078	1,081	1,117	1,159	1,354	1,486
9	Transport, storage, and communications	2,279	2,145	2,509	2,760	3,178	3,298
10	Financial intermediation	1,331	1,452	1,650	1,828	2,220	2,457
11	Real estate, renting, and business activities	2,356	2,444	2,509	2,596	2,706	2,743
12	Public administration and defense; compulsory social security	1,938	2,341	2,771	3,119	3,312	3,548
13	Education	2,849	3,174	3,756	4,417	4,906	5,597
14	Health and social work	1,426	1,517	1,436	1,812	2,036	2,247
15	Other community, social, and personal services activities	295	281	330	360	367	372
16	Private households with employed persons	74	81	93	98	102	109
	Gross Provincial Product (GPP)	31,531	35,268	41,833	47,116	47,517	54,306
	GPP per capita (ThB)	27,364	30,201	35,474	39,793	39,966	45,467
	Population (1,000 persons)	1,152	1,168	1,179	1,184	1,189	1,194

Notes: "p" indicates preliminary and "r" indicates revised.

Source: Office of the National Economic and Social Development Board, "Gross Regional and Provincial Products 2007," http://www.nesdb.go.th/Default.aspx?tabid=96.

B. Chiang Mai: Gross Provincial Product 2000–7 (ThB millions)

		2000	2002	2004	2005r	2006r	2007p
	Agriculture	8,335	13,298	11,556	13,888	15,535	17,021
1	Agriculture, hunting, and forestry	8,189	13,189	11,378	13,616	15,307	16,784
2	Fishing	147	109	177	271	228	237
	Non-agriculture	64,148	72,039	81,638	86,902	94,801	100,999
3	Mining and quarrying	575	481	636	744	868	940
4	Manufacturing	7,211	9,487	10,030	9,733	11,043	11,823
5	Electricity, gas, and water supply	1,749	1,793	2,077	2,179	2,444	2,577
6	Construction	4,234	5,259	6,260	6,730	7,089	7,379
7	Wholesale and retail trade; repair of motor vehicles, and motorcycles; and personal and household goods	12,918	14,013	15,719	16,743	17,878	18,596
8	Hotels and restaurants	7,992	8,714	10,161	11,037	12,281	13,209
9	Transport, storage, and communications	5,774	6,192	7,284	7,500	8,451	8,579
10	Financial intermediation	2,807	3,211	4,025	4,066	4,730	5,382
11	Real estate, renting, and business activities	3,684	3,983	4,277	4,455	4,678	4,832
12	Public administration and defense; compulsory social security	5,339	6,208	7,202	8,047	8,606	9,151
13	Education	7,853	7,968	7,988	9,756	10,649	12,065
14	Health and social work	3,226	3,829	4,822	4,647	4,782	5,156
15	Other community, social, and personal services activities	607	701	927	1,021	1,046	1,036
16	Private households with employed persons	179	199	230	244	256	276
	Gross Provincial Product (GPP)	72,483	85,337	93,194	100,790	110,336	118,020
	GPP per capita (ThB)	47,365	55,185	59,669	64,220	69,985	74,524
	Population (1,000 persons)	1,530	1,546	1,562	1,569	1,577	1,584

Notes: "p" indicates preliminary and "r" indicates revised.

Source: Office of the National Economic and Social Development Board, "Gross Regional and Provincial Products 2007," http://www.nesdb.go.th/Default.aspx?tabid=96.

Notes

Introduction

1. See Paul Chambers, and Eva Pascal, "Oblique Intervention: The Role of US Missionaries in Siam's Incorporation of Lanna 1867–1878," *Journal of World Christianity* 2, no. 1 (2009): 29–81.

2. Ansil Ramsay, "Modernization and Reactionary Rebellions in Northern Siam," *Journal of Asian Studies* 38, no. 2 (1979): 289; Constance M. Wilson, "The Holy Man in the History of Thailand and Laos," *Journal of Southeast Asian Studies* 28, no. 2 (1997): 345–64.

3. Joseph J. Trento, *The Secret History of the CIA* (New York: Carroll and Graf, 2005), 346.

4. Martin Booth, *Opium: A History* (New York: Thomas Dunne, 1996), 261–64.

5. Alfred McCoy, "Requiem for a Drug Lord: State and Commodity in the Career of Khun Sa," in *States and Illegal Practices*, edited by Josiah McC. Heyman, 129–68 (Oxford: Berg, 1999); Alfred McCoy, Cathleen Reed, and Leonard Adams, *The Politics of Heroin in Southeast Asia* (New York: Harper and Row, 1989).

6. Cited in Thomas Fuller, "Notorious Golden Triangle Loses Sway in the Opium Trade," *International Herald Tribune*, September 11, 2007, http://www.iht.com/articles/2007/09/11/asia/golden.php.

7. This is in the Shan State, whose opium farmers have variously claimed that this increase in cultivation is due to their poverty, the weakening of the kyat, rising prices for opium, the availability of loans for opium production, and the ease of marketing the opium. See Tom Kramer, Martin Jelsma, and Tom Blickma, *Withdrawal Symptoms in the Golden Triangle: A Drugs Market in Disarray* (Amsterdam: Transnational Institute, 2009), 22–25, available at: http://www.tni.org/report/withdrawal-symptoms-golden-triangle-4.

8. Asian Development Bank, "The GMS Program," http://www.adb.org/GMS/Program/default.asp.

9. There is an ongoing ADB technical assistance project to evaluate the impact of NSEC: ADB, "Development Study of GMS Economic Corridors" (RETA6310).

10. In Chiang Rai Province, besides the permanent checkpoints of Mae Sai, Chiang Khong, and Chiang Saen, there are four additional exempt crossing points between Thailand and Myanmar as well as four other exempt crossing points

between Thailand and Laos. "Exempt" alludes to the fact that the points are often closed but reopen occasionally by mutual agreement.

11. Andrew Walker, *The Legend of the Golden Boat: Regulation, Trade and Traders in the Borderlands of Laos, Thailand, China, and Burma* (Honolulu: University of Hawai'i Press, 1999), 186–93.

12. Kuah Khun Eng, "Negotiating Policies: Border Trading in Southern China," in *Where China Meets Southeast Asia: Social and Cultural Change in the Border Regions*, edited by Grant Evans, et al. (Singapore: ISEAS, 2000), 95.

13. Chen Xiangming, *As Borders Bend: Transnational Spaces on the Pacific Rim* (Lanham: Rowman & Littlefield, 2005).

14. Shalmali Guttal, "An Investor's Paradise: Trade in the Mekong Region," *Focus on the Global South*, March 2006, http://www.focusweb.org/an-investor-s-paradise-trade-in-the-mekong-region.html.

Chapter 1: Postclassical Realism and Subregional Economic Zones

1. For a pathbreaking exposition of liberalism (pluralism), see Robert O. Keohane and Joseph Nye, *Power and Interdependence: World Politics in Transition* (Boston: Little, Brown, 1977).

2. See, for instance, Kenichi Ohmae, *The Borderless World: Power and Strategy in the Interlinked Economy* (New York: HarperBusiness, 1990).

3. *The Next Global Stage: Challenges and Opportunities in Our Borderless World* (Upper Saddle River, NJ: Wharton, 2005).

4. Kenichi Ohmae, *The End of the Nation State: The Rise of Regional Economies* (New York: Free Press, 1995), 143.

5. Ibid., 89.

6. Paul Hirst and Grahame Thompson, *Globalization in Question: The International Economy and the Possibilities of Governance* (Cambridge, Mass.: Wiley-Blackwell, 1999), 88.

7. See Friedrich E. Kratochwil and John Gerard Ruggie, "International Organization: A State of the Art on an Art of the State," *International Organization* 40 (1986): 753–75.

8. Jeffrey T. Checkel, "Social Construction and Integration," Advanced Research on the Europeanisation of the Nation-State (ARENA) Working Paper 98/14 (Oslo: ARENA, 1998).

9. See Alexander Wendt, "Collective Identity Formation and the International State," *American Political Science Review* 88, no. 2, 1994: 384–96.

10. Peter M. Haas, "Introduction: Epistemic Communities and International Policy Coordination," *International Organization* 46 (1992): 3.

11. Jörn Dosch, "Managing Security in ASEAN-China Relations: Liberal Peace or Hegemonic Stability," *Asian Perspective* 31, no. 1 (2007): 227.

12. Ibid.

13. Stephen Walt, "International Relations: One World, Many Theories," in "Frontiers of Knowledge," special edition, *Foreign Policy* 110 (Spring 1998): 29–46.

14. See Karl Marx, *Capital: An Abridged Edition*, edited by David McLellan (Oxford: Oxford Paperbacks, 2008).

15. Paul Viotti and Mark Kauppi, *International Relations Theory: Realism, Pluralism, Globalism, and Beyond* (Boston: Allyn and Bacon, 1999), 474.

16. Immanuel Wallerstein, "Patterns and Perspectives of the Capitalist World Economy," *Contemporary Marxism* 9 (1984): 59–70.

17. See Immanuel Wallerstein, *The Modern World-System: Capitalist Agriculture and the Origins of the European World-Economy in the Sixteenth Century* (New York: Academic Press, 1976), 231–33.

18. See Antonio Gramsci, *Selections from the Prison Notebooks*, translated and edited by Quintin Hoare and Geoffrey Nowell Smith (New York: International Publishers, 1971), 1–2.

19. Craig Murphy, "Freezing the North-South Bloc(k) after the East–West Thaw," *Socialist Review* 20, no. 3 (1990): 25–46.

20. For a general examination of realism, see Viotti and Kauppi, *International Relations Theory*, chapter 2.

21. See Kenneth Waltz, *Theory of International Politics* (New York: McGraw-Hill, 1979); Kenneth Waltz, "Realist Thought and Neorealist Theory," *Journal of International Affairs* 44, no. 1 (1990): 21–38.

22. Robert O. Keohane, "International Institutions: Two Approaches," *International Studies Quarterly* 32, no. 4 (1988): 384.

23. See Alfred Oehlers, "A Critique of ADB Policies toward the Greater Mekong Sub-region," *Journal of Contemporary Asia* 36, no. 4 (2006): 464–79.

24. Robert O. Keohane, "Neoliberal Institutionalism: A Perspective on World Politics," in *International Institutions and State Power: Essays in International Relations Theory*, edited by Robert Keohane (Boulder, Co.: Westview, 1989), 2.

25. UNESCAP, *Greater Mekong Subregion Business Handbook* (New York: United Nations, 2002), 1.

26. See, for instance, Viotti and Kauppi, *International Relations Theory*, 216.

27. See Stephen Brooks, "Dueling Realisms," *International Organization* 51, no. 3 (1997): 445–77. For other applications of postclassical realism, see Paul Chambers, "Harnessing Suwannaphum: Thailand's Foreign Economic Policy toward Mainland Southeast Asia in the Era of Thaksin," in *Bureaucracy and National Security in Southeast Asia: Essays in Honor of M. Ladd Thomas*, edited by Daniel H. Unger and Clark D. Neher, 131–61 (DeKalb: Northern Illinois University Press, 2006); Paul Chambers, "Edgy Amity along the Mekong: Thai-Lao Relations in a Transforming Regional Equilibrium," *Asian Journal of Political Science* 17, no.

1 (2009): 89–118; Tsuyoshi Kawasaki, "Post-Classical Realism and Japanese Security Policy," *Pacific Review* 14, no. 2 (2001): 221–40.

28. Unlike postclassical realism, neoclassical realism is a variant of realism focusing on the domestic levels of analysis. See Gideon Rose, "Neoclassical Realism and Theories of Foreign Policy," *World Politics* 51, no. 1 (1998): 144–72.

29. Brooks, "Dueling Realisms," 463.

30. Ibid., 446.

31. Military security is defined as state defensive capabilities while the *2005 Human Security Report* defines human security as the protection of individuals and communities from any form of political violence (http://www. humansecurityreport.info/). The human security referred to in this study is that of refugees and migrant labor.

32. Brooks, "Dueling Realisms," 462.

33. Barth argues that an "economic dilemma model" of security can be intertwined with postclassical realism. See Aharon Barth, "Econo-Realism: Putting Economics at Center Stage: How Does, and Should, IR Research React to Expanding Economic Interdependence?," paper presented at the International Studies Association, 41st Annual Convention, Los Angeles, March 14–18, 2000, https:// www.ciaonet.org/isa/baa01/.

34. Brooks, "Dueling Realisms," 455–58.

35. Robert Gilpin, *War and Change in World Politics* (Cambridge: Cambridge University Press, 1981), 13–14.

36. Brooks, "Dueling Realisms," 471–72.

37. Ibid., 467.

38. By "weak," I mean that Laos has both fragile economic and minor military capabilities. According to the *2006 United Nations Development Program Report*, it remains one of the least developed and poorest countries in the world. See also the World Bank, *Lao Economic Monitor* 2006, http://lnweb18.worldbank.org/eap/eap. nsf/Attachments/LaoPDR+EcMonitor0403/$File/LaoPDR+EcMon0403.pdf). Lao's military is considered "small, poorly funded, and ineffectively resourced," Central Intelligence Agency, *World Factbook*, 2010, https://www.cia.gov/library/ publications/the-world-factbook/geos/la.html.

39. Paul Battersby, "Border Politics and the Broader Politics of Thailand's International Relations in the 1990s: From Communism to Capitalism," *Pacific Affairs* 71, no. 4 (1998–1999): 473–88.

40. Ibid., 487–88.

41. The ASEAN member-states are Brunei, Cambodia, Indonesia, Laos, Thailand, Malaysia, Myanmar, the Philippines, Singapore, and Vietnam. The signing of the ASEAN Charter in 2007 gave the group a legal identity and turns it into a more effective and cohesive organization after four decades of existence. Mergawati Zulfakar, "ASEAN Charter Inked," *The Star*, November 20, 2007, 1.

42. See James Mittleman, "Rethinking the International Division of Labour in the Context of Globalisation," *Third World Quarterly* 16, no. 2 (1995): 273–95.

43. Patrick Taran and Eduardo Geronimi, "Globalization, Labor and Migration: Protection is Paramount," paper presented at the Conferencia Hemisférica sobre Migración Internacional: Derechos Humanos y Trata de Personas en las Américas, Santiago de Chile, November 20–22, 2002, 5.

Chapter 2: Thailand's Role in Regionalism and GMS Border Trade

1. Shalmali Guttal, "Marketing the Mekong: The Asian Development Bank and the Greater Mekong Sub-region Economic Cooperation Program," *Jubilee South*, December 12, 2003. http://www.jubileesouth.org/news/EpZyVyEAZFESZsvoiN. shtml.

2. UNESCAP, *Greater Mekong Subregion Business Handbook* (New York: United Nations, 2002), 1.

3. See, for instance, Noam Chomsky, *Profit over People: Neo-liberalism and Global Order* (New York: Seven Stories Press, 1999); Craig Murphy, *Global Institutions, Marginalization, and Development* (London: Routledge/RIPE Studies in Global Political Economy, 2005).

4. Thein Swe and Paul Chambers, "Political Economy on the Perimeter: State Policy and Trade on Thailand's Border with Myanmar and Laos," paper presented at the 10th International Thai Studies Conference, Thammasat University, Bangkok, January 9–11, 2008, 53–57.

5. Meenakshi S. S. Sundaram, *Decentralisation in Developing Countries* (New Delhi: Concept Publishing, 1994), 11.

6. Michel Foucault, *Power/Knowledge: Selected Interviews and Other Writings, 1992–97*, edited by C. Gordon (New York: Pantheon, 1980).

7. Interview with Pattana Sittisombat, Chairman, Chiang Rai Chambers of Commerce, April 20, 2007; interview with Somchai Sirisujin, Chiang Mai Chamber of Commerce, June 10, 2008.

8. Glassman, "Recovering from Crisis," 364;, Jim Glassman and Chris Sneddon, "Chiang Mai and Khon Kaen as Growth Poles: Regional Industrial Development in Thailand and its Implications for Urban Sustainability," *Annals of the American Academy of Political and Social Science* 590, no. 1 (2003): 109–111; Jim Glassman, *Thailand at the Margins: Internationalization of the State and the Transformation of Labour* (Oxford: Oxford University Press, 2004).

9. Alex Mutebi, "Recentralising while Decentralising: Centre-Local Relations and 'CEO' Governors in Thailand," *Asia-Pacific Journal of Public Administration* 26, no. 1 (June 2004): 33–53.

10. While this subject is beyond the scope of this study, there is a substantial literature on decentralization in Thailand including: Daniel Arghiros, *Democracy, Development and Decentralization in Provincial Thailand* (Richmond: Curzon Press, 2001); Michael H. Nelson, "Thailand: Problems with Decentralization?" In

Thailand's New Politics: KPI Yearbook 2001, edited by Michael H. Nelson, 219–81 (Nonthaburi and Bangkok: King Prajadhipok's Institute and White Lotus Press, 2002); Michael H. Nelson, "Analyzing Provincial Political Structures in Thailand: *phuak*, *trakun*, and *hua khanaen*," SEARC Working Paper Series, no. 78 (Hong Kong: Southeast Asia Research Centre, City University of Hong Kong, 2005), http://www.cityu.edu.hk/searc.

11. George Abonyi, "Activity-based Regional Cooperation in Asia," paper prepared for ADB workshop, 2003, 17–18, http://www.adbi.org/files/2003.12.10.cpp.activity.based.cooperation.pdf.

12. Songpol Kaopatumtip and Siriporn Sachamuneewongse, "Shaking up the Neighborhood," *Bangkok Post*, May 4, 2008, http://www.bangkokpost.com.

13. Ibid.

14. "Chinese–Myanmar Economic Ties Continue to Strengthen," *Myanmar Times*, December 31, 2007–January 6, 2008, http://www.mmtimes.com/no399/b005.htm.

15. ADB, *Key Indicators for Asia and the Pacific 2008*, http://www.adb.org/statistics.

16. "Route Completed Linking S. China with N. Thailand Via Laos," Xinhua, March 31, 2008, available at: http://www.chinadaily.com.cn/china/2008-03/31/content_6579704.htm.

17. Asian Development Bank, "Loan 1989 to Laos, Greater Mekong Subregion: Northern Economic Corridor Project," http://www.adb.org/GMS/projects/loan-1989.asp. The total length of the project road is 228 kilometers, of which the northern section of about 69 kilometers will be funded by People's Repubic of China, the central section of 74 kilometers will be funded by ADB, and the southern section of about 85 kilometers will be funded by Thailand. See also other ADB documents related to the loan, including the "Report and Recommendation of the President" (RRP: LAO 34321 November 2002).

18. Vatthana Pholsena and Ruth Banomyong, *Laos: From Buffer State to Crossroads?* (Chiang Mai: Mekong Press, 2006), 122.

19. Theerawat Khamthita, "From Chiang Rai to China via Burma: New Transnational Road Due for Completion within Two Weeks," *Bangkok Post*, January 14, 2004, http://www.bangkokpost.com.

20. Estimates based on information gleaned from Thailand's Ministry of Industry, NESDB, and Ministry of Labor. See Takao Tsuneishi, "The Regional Development Policy of Thailand and its Economic Cooperation with Neighboring Countries," Institute of Developing Economies (IDE) Discussion Paper no. 32, 2005 (Chiba: IDE-JETRO). Investment figures are from BOI (compiled by Bank of Thailand).

21. Liu and Xiong, "Strategic Development of Logistics Cooperation."

22. Liu Jinxin and Xiong Bin, "Strategic Development of Logistics Cooperation between Yunnan, China and Northern Thailand," paper presented at the "Logistics Development in the Greater Mekong Sub-region" Conference, March 18–19, 2008, US Commercial Service, Shangri-La Hotel, Chiang Mai, http://www.buyusa.gov/thailand/en/logistics.html.

23. Tanit Sorat (Secretary General, Federation of Thai Industries, President of V-Serve Group), "Thailand Cross Border Logistics," paper presented at the "Logistics Development in the Greater Mekong Sub-region" Conference, US Commercial Service, Shangri-La Hotel, Chiang Mai, March 18–19, 2008, http://www.buyusa.gov/thailand/en/logistics.html.

24. Interview with Kevin J. Rosier, May 8, 2008.

25. Siriluk, "Sino-Thai Strategic Development," 307.

26. Tsuneishi, "The Regional Development Policy of Thailand," 18–19.

27. All GMS countries aim to reconcile customs procedures and raise them to international standards, according to Sathit Limpongpan, director-general of the Thai Customs Department.

28. Bangkok has streamlined trade procedures in other ways: business registration time is being shortened; most export licensing requirements are being phased out; imports of raw materials are now approved on an annual plan basis rather than shipment by shipment; trade legislation has been revised to increase transparency and predictability and generally facilitate business and trade; and foreign (Thai) transporters can now deliver goods directly to their final destination in Laos. UNESCAP, "Trade Facilitation in the Greater Mekong Subregion," In *Trade and Investment Division Report 2007*, 65, http://www.unescap.org/tid/publication/chap9_2224.pdf.

29. Wichit Chaitrong, "Mekong States Meet on Customs," *The Nation*, September 15, 2006, http://www.nationmultimedia.com.

30. Don Pathan, "Greater Mekong Subregion Moves Closer," *The Nation*, July 5, 2005, http://www.nationmultimedia.com.

31. Porametee Vimolsiri, "Thailand as a Transport Hub for the Greater Mekong Subregion," NESDB, 2007, http://www.nesdb.go.th-Portals-0-home-interest-Thailand as a Transport Hub.pdf.

32. Jonathan Hopfner, "Fast Times," *Globe and Mail*, January 10, 2004, T1, http://www.globeandmail.com.

33. Mekong River Commission, *The People's Highway: Past, Present and Future Transport on the Mekong River System* (Vientiane: MRC Secretariat, 2003), 26.

34. Kosum Saichan, "ASEAN +3 and GMS: Case Studies of Regional Integration," Case Studies of Regional Integration," in *Contemporary Global Issues in Social Sciences*, edited by Usamad Siampakdee (Chiang Mai: Chiang Mai University, 2005), 64.

35. A special economic zones (SEZ) law was formally enacted in Myanmar by the end of 2007. Under the law, Myanmar designated six cities as zones: Thilawa Port in Yangon, Mawlamyine in Mon State, Myawaddy and Hpa-an in Kayin State, Kyaukphyu in Rakhine State, and Pyin Oo Lwin in Mandalay Division. This includes three Thai-proposed special industrial zones, located in Myawaddy and Hpa-an in southeastern Kayin State and Mawlamyine in southern Mon State. The project constitutes part of the ACMECS program. See "Roundup: Myanmar on Road to Establishing Special Economic Zones," Xinhua March 13, 2007, http://english.people.com.cn/200703/13/eng20070313_357029.html.

36. Petchanet Pratruangkrai, "ACMECS Cooperation: 50% Rise in Mekong Region Trade Expected," *The Nation*, October 13, 2005, http://www.nationmultimedia.com.

37. The Chiang Rai Zone derived from the NESDB Strategic Plan for the Upper North (1999–2008) to further develop this region by improving its trade linkages with China.

38. Siriluk Masviriyakul, "Sino-Thai Strategic Development in the Greater Mekong Subregion (1992–2003)," *Contemporary Southeast Asia* 26, no. 2 (2004): 307.

39. Somphong Wanapha, "The Shifting Paradigm of FDI Policy and Promotion in Thailand," paper presented at the Global Forum on International Investment: Attracting Foreign Investment for Development, Organization for Economic Cooperation and Development, Shanghai, December 5–6, 2002, http://www.oecd.org/dataoecd/54/63/2764564.pdf.

40. Jim Glassman, "Recovering from Crisis: The Case of Thailand's Spatial Fix," *Economic Geography* 83, no. 4 (2007): 353, 364.

41. Walden Bello, "China and Southeast Asia: Emerging Problems in an Economic Relationship," *People Before Profit*, http://www.globalmon.org.hk/en/china_reports/200612waldenbello.html.

42. Ibid.

43. The OAE data as well as the argument made derives from Andrew Walker, " A Flood of Chinese Garlic," *New Mandala: New Perspectives on Mainland Southeast Asia* (blog), October 24, 2007, http://asiapacific.anu.edu.au/newmandala/2007/10/24/a-flood-of-chinese-garlic/.

44. Bello, "China and Southeast Asia."

45. Petchanet Patruangkrai, "Non-Tariff Barriers with China Attacked," *The Nation*, May 26, 2007, http://www.nationmultimedia.com.

46. "China, ASEAN Sign Trade in Services Agreement of FTA," Xinhua, January 15, 2007, http://www.bilaterals.org/article.php3?id_article=6917&var_recherche=ASEAN-China.

47. Nadia Saccardo, "China: Targeted for In-bound FDI," 2005, http://www.Business-in-Asia.com.

48. Mandala Sukarto Purba, "Towards Regionalism through the ASEAN-China Free Trade Area: Prospects and Challenges," Master's thesis, University of the West Cape, May 2006, http://etd.uwc.ac.za/usrfiles/modules/etd/docs/etd_gen8Srv25Nme4_9213_1183461348.pdf, 19.

49. Saccardo, "China."

50. Petchanet, "Non-Tariff Barriers with China Attacked."

51. Bannop Tangsriwong and Akekarat Bangleng, "A New Silk Road?" *Thai Asia Today*, December 10, 2007, http://www.Thaiasiatoday.com.

52. Guangxi Zhuang Autonomous Region, China, acceded to the GMS in 2005.

53. See David S. G. Goodman, ed., *China's Campaign to "Open the West": National, Provincial, and Local* Perspectives, Special Issue, *China Quarterly* (Cambridge: Cambridge University Press, 2004).

54. Hisane Masaki, "China, Japan Tug-of-War over Indochina," *Asia Times Online*, 2005, http://www.atimes.com/atimes/Japan/GJ05Dh03.html.

55. See Nitida Asawanipont, "Partner and Competitor: VN Offers Great Opportunities, but Will Be a Fierce Rival," *The Nation*, August 14, 2006, http://www.nationmultimedia.com.

56. "Vietnam vs. Thailand: Competitors in Trade-Investment-Tourism," May 3, 2006, Kasikorn Research Centre, http://www.kasikornresearch.com/kr/eng/search_detail.jsp?id=5527&cid=11.

57. Asian Development Bank, *Outlook 2008 Update*, http://www.adb.org/Documents/Books/ADO/2008/Update/Part03-VIE.pdf.

58. Derived from a study by Pornsak Phongphaew of Chulalongkorn University entitled "The Casinos along the Thai Border: Effects and Guidelines to Solutions," which was submitted to Thailand's Anti-Money Laundering Office (AMLO). See "Gamblers will Gamble," *Bangkok Post*, November 10, 2002, http://www.bangkokpost.com.

59. "Gambling on the Greater Good," *Bangkok Post*, November 17, 2002, http://www.bangkokpost.com.

60. Sai Soe Win Latt, "What if Thailand Wants 'Migrant Problems'?" *Irrawaddy*, July 14, 2008, http://www.irrawaddy.org/opinion_story.php?art_id=13315.

61. Bryant Yuan Fu Yang, "Life and Death away from the Golden Land: The Plight of Burmese Migrant Workers in Thailand," *Thailand Law Journal* 1, no. 12 (Spring 2009), http://www.thailawforum.com/Volume12Spring%2009.html.

62. Ibid.

63. International Organization for Migration (IOM), "Migration in South East Asia," 2009, http://www.iom-seasia.org/index.php?module=pagesetter&func=printpub&tid=6&pid=284.

64. Sai, "What if Thailand Wants 'Migrant Problems'?"

65. He Jinsong, "Myanmar Migrant Workers in Thailand: Policies and Prospects," *Asian Scholar* 5 (2007), http://www.asianscholarship.org/asf/ejourn/articles/he_j.pdf. 11.

66. Thai Ministry of Labor figures cited in He, "Myanmar Migrant Workers," 2.

67. IOM, "Labor Migration."

68. IOM, "Laos," 2009, http://www.iom-seasia.org/index.php?module=pagesetter&func=viewpub&tid=6&pid=46.

69. See Andrew Walker, "Regional Trade in Northwestern Laos: An Initial Assessment of the Economic Triangle," in *Where China Meets Southeast Asia: Social and Cultural Change in the Border Regions*, edited by Grant Evans, Christopher Hutton, and Kuah Khun Eng (Singapore: ISEAS, 2000), 142.

70. Interview with Pattana Sittisombat.

Chapter 3: Border Trade between Myanmar and Thailand at Tachilek-Mae Sai

1. "Roundup: Myanmar takes Measures to Boost Border Trade with Neighboring Countries," Xinhua, August 2, 2006, http://www.indoburmanews.net/archives-1/archive06/aug_06/neighboring/; Myanmar-Thai bilateral trade hit over $2 bln in eight months of 2008–09," Xinhua, January 8, 2009, http://news.xinhuanet.com/english/2009–01/30/content_10736297.htm.

2. "New Schweli River Crossing Opens," Shan Herald Agency for News, September 19, 2005, http://www.shanland.org/general/2005/Shweli-river.

3. Interview with fifth group of anonymous merchants in Mae Sai, Thailand, June 21, 2007.

4. Conclusions based upon study team member Jinhui Lai's interviews with various anonymous Chinese businesspeople in Mae Sai, Thailand, July 21, 2007.

5. Interview with Somchai Sirisujin (former Chairman of the Chiang Mai Chamber of Commerce), March 22, 2007.

6. "Thai-Myanmar Border Trade Resumes amid Fanfare," Reuters, September 16, 1998, http://www.burmalibrary.org/reg.burma/archives/199809/msg00519.html.

7. Interview with Kiatchai Bhongprapai, Chief Customs Inspector, Mae Sai Customs House, October 15, 2007.

8. "Border Checkpoints Reopen to Little Fanfare," The Nation, October 16, 2002, http://www.nationmultimedia.com.

9. Interview with Kiatchai Bhongprapai.

10. Theerawat Khamthita, "From Chiang Rai to China via Burma: New Transnational Road Due for Completion within Two Weeks," Bangkok Post, January 14, 2004, http://www.bangkokpost.com.

11. David Fullbrook, "Thailand in China's Embrace," Asia Times Online, April 9, 2004, http://www.atimes.com/atimes/Southeast_Asia/FD09Ae04.html.

12. Siriluk Masviriyakul, "Sino-Thai Strategic Development in the Greater Mekong Subregion (1992–2003)," Contemporary Southeast Asia 26, no. 2 (2004): 308.

13. Don Pathan, "Greater Mekong Subregion Moves Closer," The Nation, July 5, 2005, http://www.nationmultimedia.com.

14. "Myanmar to Partly Retain Border Trade System in Second Border Trade Zone," People's Daily Online, September 6, 2006, http://english.people.com.cn/200609/06/eng20060906_299848.html.

15. Sopaporn Saeung, "Second Bridge to Burma Opens in Mae Sai," The Nation, January 23, 2006, http://www.nationmultimedia.com.

16. "Second Friendship Bridge to Burma at Mae Sai Border in Chiang Mai," Chiang Mai Mail, January 28–February 3, 2006, http://www.chiangmai-mail.com/171/news.shtml#hd5.

17. Clive Parker, "Straining to Bridge the Divide," Irrawaddy, February 10, 2006, http://www.irrawaddy.org/aviewer.asp?a=5451&z=104.

18. Saksit Meesubkwang, "Burmese Authorities Permit Teak Imports," *Chiang Mai Mail* August 19–25, 2006, http://www.chiangmai-mail.com/200/news.shtml# hd9. See also chapter 7.

19. "Irrawaddy: Fifty Customs Officials Arrested in New Policy Sweep," November 29, 2006, http://www.burmanet.org.

20. "PM Urged to Press Burma to Open Trade," *Bangkok Post*, November 17, 2006, http://www.bangkokpost.com.

21. "China Pursues More Blasting of Reefs," *Bangkok Post*, December 21, 2006, http//www.bangkokpost.com.

22. Myanmar-Thai Bilateral Trade up over 50 Percent in 2006–07," http://english.people.com; "Myanmar-Thai Bilateral Trade Hit over $2 bln in Eight Months of 2008–09," Xinhua, January 8, 2009, http://english.peopledaily.com.

23. *Weekly Eleven News*, March 17, 2010, 5.

24. Bank of Thailand, "EC_XT_003:Trade Classified by Country (US$)," http://www.bot.or.th/English/Statistics/EconomicAndFinancial/ExternalSector/Pages/StatInternationalTrade.aspx.

25. Aung Htet, "Thailand Marks Trade Deficit with Burma," *Irrawaddy*, June 18, 2007, http://www.irrawaddymedia.com.

26. Aung Htet, "Thailand Marks Trade Deficit with Burma"; "Thailand's First Trade Deficit with Burma," *Bangkok Post*, June 18, 2007, http://www.bangkokpost.com; "Burma Uncertain Trade Policy Leads to Decline of Imports from Thailand," Mungpi, Mizzima News, http://www.com/MizzimaNews/News/2007/June/39–June-2007.html.

27. "Thailand's First Trade Deficit with Burma."

28. Chen Xiangming, *As Borders Bend: Transnational Spaces on the Pacific Rim* (New York: Rowman & Littlefield, 2005).

29. Conclusions based upon study team member Jinhui Lai's interviews with various anonymous Chinese businesspeople in Mae Sai, Thailand, July 21, 2007.

30. Interview with first group of anonymous merchants interviewed in Tachilek, July 21, 2007.

31. Interview with third group of anonymous merchants in Mae Sai, July 21, 2007.

32. Ibid.

33. Ibid.

34. Ibid.

35. Ibid.

36. Interview with Kiatchai Bhongprapai.

37. There is a lack of reliable data on the relative percentage of LPG and crude petroleum products in Myanmar's total exports.

38. Thomas Kean, "Kyaukphyu–Yunnan Oil Pipeline to be Completed by End of 2015," *Myanmar Times*, November 30–December 6, 2009, http://mmtimes.com/no499/no13.htm; Roberta Quadrelli, "ASEAN Statistics by the International Energy Agency," paper presented at the Training Session on Emergency Preparedness and

Statistics, Paris, February 11–14, 2008, http://www.iea.org/work/2008/asean_training/Quadrelli.pdf.

39. "Myanmar to Host Four-Country Commercial Navigation Meeting," Xinhua, April 5, 2007, http://www.english.people.com.cn/200704/05/eng20070405_363989.html.

40. Interview with On Unthaweesup, Mae Sai Customs House, March 30, 2008.

41. Interview with fifth group of anonymous merchants in Mae Sai, Thailand, June 21, 2007.

42. Supradit Kanwanich, "Gamblers will Gamble," *Bangkok Post*, November 10, 2002, http://www.bangkokpost.com.

43. "Survey on Industrial Co-operation between Myanmar and Thailand: A Study Report for JODC," *Myanmar News*, March 2004, http://www.allmyanmar.com.

44. "Thai–Burma Relations Burma Opens Wider Door for Gamblers," *Burma News International*, January 21, 2005, http://burmalibrary.org/docs3/BNI2005–01-22.htm.

Chapter 4: From Mae Sai to Mongla

1. Interview with anonymous Myanmar businessman, Tachilek, Myanmar, September 25, 2008.

2. "Lin Moves Casinos Out," Shan Herald Agency for News, April 9, 2006, http://www.shanland.org/drugs/2006/News-02090406/?searchterm=sai%20lin.

3. "Road Construction in Shan State: A Lucrative Way to Turn Illegal Drug Profits into Legal Revenues," *Undercurrents: Monitoring Development on Burma's Mekong*, Lahu National Development Organization, 12–13, http://www.shanland.org/resources/bookspub/humanrights/UNDERCURRENTS.pdf.

4. Lahu National Development Organization, "Aftershocks along Burma's Mekong," *Burma Library*, 2004, http://burmalibrary.org/docs/AFTERSHOCKS%20ALONG%20BURMA.htm; "Road Construction in Shan State"; "Law and Wei Win Road Construction Contracts," Shan Herald News Agency, 2001, http://www.shanland.org/drugs/2001/law_and_wei_win_road_constructio.htm/.

5. Interview with anonymous Myanmar businessman, Mongla, September 26, 2008.

6. "Chinese Police Invade Burma," Shan Herald Agency for News, 2005, http://www.shanland.org/general/2005/Chinese-police-invades-Burma/?searchterm=mongla.

7. Michael Black and Roland Fields, "Virtual Gambling in Myanmar's Drug Country," *Asia Times Online*, August 27, 2006, http://www.atimesonline.com.

8. "Mongla Casinos Doomed but That's No Big Deal," *Burma News International*, http://www.bnionline.net/index.php?option=com_content&task=view&id=3745&Itemid=6.

9. Interview with massage girls, Tianshun Massage Shop, Mongla, September 26, 2008.

10. Ibid.

11. Interview with anonymous Myanmar businessman, Mongla, September 25, 2008. Actual figures are difficult to determine for reasons discussed elsewhere.
12. According to Myanmar expert Dr. Ron Renard, despite Myanmar's campaign against opium production, the level of such production has returned to 1986 levels. Interview with Ron Renard, September 18, 2008.
13. Interview with second group of anonymous merchants in Tachilek, July 21, 2007.
14. Interview with anonymous Myanmar businessman, Mongla, September 26, 2008.
15. Authors' own observations and interview with anonymous Myanmar businessman, Tachilek, September 28, 2008.
16. Interview with anonymous local Myanmar driver, Kengtung, September 26, 2008.
17. "Energy Projects: Chinese Make Move: MDX, Ratchaburi Face Threat in Huge Power Schemes," *The Nation*, November 21, 2007, http://nationmultimedia. com/2007/11/21/business/business_30056827.php.
18. Estimated at the market rate of ThB1.00 = kyats 28.00, though it should be remembered that the kyat is overvalued by Myanmar. Lahu National Development Organization, "Aftershocks."
19. Lahu National Development Organization, "Aftershocks."
20. Fredrich Kahrl, Su Yufang, and Horst Weyerhaeuser, "Navigating the Border: An Analysis of the China-Myanmar Timber Trade" (Washington, D.C.: Forest Trends, 2004), 4.
21. Lahu National Development Organization, "Aftershocks."
22. "Mongla will not be Pushed," August 22, 2006, Shan Herald Agency for News, http://www.burmanet.org/news/2006/08/22/shan-herald-agency-for-news-mongla-will-not-be-pushed/.
23. Lahu National Development Organization, "Aftershocks."
24. Interview with fourth group of anonymous merchants in Mae Sai, June 21, 2007.

Chapter 5: Border Trade between Laos and Thailand via Houayxay-Chiang Khong

1. "Thailand and Laos: Cooperation Enhancing Mutual Prosperity," Kasikorn Research Centre, March 19, 2004, http://www.kasikornresearch.com.
2. "Laos Demands Licenses for Border Trade," October 24, 2007, *Bangkok Post*, http://www.bangkokpost.com.
3. Interview with Sanguan Sonklinsakul, Chiang Khong representative of the Chiang Rai Chamber of Commerce, May 5, 2007.
4. Interview with Sanguan Sonklinsakul, 2007; interview with Pattana Sittisombat, Chairman of the Chiang Rai Chamber of Commerce, June 11, 2007.
5. See table B in the appendix; interview with Sanguan Sonklinsakul.

6. Anoma Srisukkasem, "Thai-Lao Border Commerced: BOT Moves to Facilitate Trade," *The Nation*, August 18, 2004, http://www.nationmultimedia.com.

7. Johanna Son, "Open Borders Expose Mekong's Disparities," Inter Press Service (IPS) News, February 10, 2007, http://www.ipsnews.net/news.

8. Interview with Pattana Sittisombat.

9. "Thai-Lao Agreement on Currency to Help Trade," *Financial Times*, August 18, 2004, http://www.financialtimes.com.

10. Interview with Sanguan Sonklinsakul.

11. Interview with Sanguan Sonklinsakul.

12. "Laos Demands Licenses for Border Trade".

13. Interview with Pattana Sittisombat.

14. Interview with Chiang Khong Deputy Mayor Tirayudh, June 11, 2007.

15. "Thailand and Laos: Cooperation Enhancing Mutual Prosperity," Kasikorn Research Center, March 19, 2004, http://www.kasikornresearch.com/kr/eng/search_detail. jsp?id=1905&cid=14.

16. Saksit Meesubkwang, "As the River Dies, Chiang Rai MPs Oppose Dams and New Port, *Chiang Mail Mail*, June 11–17, 2005, http://www.chiangmai-mail.com.

17. Interview with Pattana Sittisombat.

18. "A Route to Prosperity," *Bangkok Post*, March 29, 2008, http://www.bangkokpost. com.

19. "Construction of Fourth Lao-Thai Bridge to Start in March," *The Nation*, January 15, 2010, http://www.nationmultimedia.com.

20. "Construction of a New Thai-Lao Friendship Bridge," Government Public Relations Department, March 16, 2007, http://www.thailand.prd.go.th.

21. "Premier Wen Makes Proposals on Boosting Co-op in GMS," GOV.cn: Chinese Government's Official Website, March 31, 2008, http://english.gov.cn/2008-03/31/content_933280.htm.

22. Interview with Sanguan Sonklinsakul.

23. "Naowarat Suksamran, "New Thai-Lao Bridge Throws up Old Problems," *Bangkok Post*, April 23, 2007, http://www.bangkokpost.com; confirmed in interview with Sanguan Sonklinsakul.

24. Naowarat, "New Thai-Lao Bridge Throws up Old Problems."

25. Naowarat Suksamran and Subin Kheunkaew, "A Bridge Too Far: Many Local Residents are Still Not Convinced the Project Will Take Off," *Bangkok Post*, February 18, 2007, http://www.bangkokpost.com.

26. Naowarat, "New Thai-Lao Bridge Throws up Old Problems"; Theerawat Khamthita, "Industrial Estate Move Confirmed," *Bangkok Post*, January 12, 2005, http://www.bangkokpost.com.

27. "Chinese Open B1Bn Hotel in Chiang Rai Near Laos Border," *Bangkok Post*, December 12, 2007, http://www.bangkokpost.com.

28. Interview with Chiang Khong Deputy Mayor Tirayudh.

29. Interview with Sanguan Sonklinsakul.

30. Interview with Sanguan Sonklinsakul.

31. Interview with Sanguan Sonklinsakul.
32. Interview with Chiang Khong Deputy Mayor Tirayudh, June 11, 2007.
33. Quoted in Naowarat Suksamran, "New Thai-Lao Bridge Throws up Old Problems."
34. Interview with Sanguan Sonklinsakul.
35. Authors' observation, June 28, 2008.
36. Interviews with two separate cell-phone shopowners in Houayxay, June 28, 2008.
37. Interview with the owner of a guesthouse in Houayxay, June 28, 2008.
38. Interview with the owner of a Beer Lao distribution company in Houayxay, June 28, 2008.
39. Interview with "Mekong Lao Restaurant" manager, Houayxay, June 27, 2008.

Chapter 6: From Chiang Khong to China

1. Thomas Fuller, "Kunming-Bangkok," *International Herald Tribune*, March 30, 2008, http://www.iht.com.
2. "China Section of Kunming-Bangkok Highway Completed," Xinhua, March 22, 2008, available at http://www.chinadaily.com.cn/bizchina/2008-03/22/content_content_6557918.htm; Anucha Charoenpo, "Prime Ministers Open New Highway to China," *Bangkok Post*, http://www.bangkokpost.com.
3. Asian Development Bank, "TAR: Lao 34231, Technical Assistance (Financed from the Japan Special Fund) to the Lao People's Democratic Republic for Preparing the Northern Economic Corridor Project" (Manila: ADB, December 2001), http://www.adb.org/Documents/TARs/LAO/r12_02.pdf.
4. In March 2003, Laos granted VPL a concession to explore for and mine lignite in Vieng Phoukha district in Luang Namtha Province in an area of 108 square kilometers. VPL has a 20-year mining concession extendable every ten years. VPL aims to build a power generation plant to produce raw materials for Thailand's battery industry and to develop land for commercial use and tourism. See Embassy of the Lao PDR to the United States of America, "Investment Opportunities and Selected Potentially Attractive Sectors," available at http://www.business-in-asia.com/laos.htm.
5. "Investment Opportunities and Selected Potentially Attractive Sectors."
6. Naowarat Suksamran, "New Thai-Lao Bridge Throws up Old Problems."
7. Author's interview with anonymous Laemthong Company official, Chiang Khong, March 31, 2008; author's interview with anonymous Lao businessman, Houayxay, April 19, 2008.
8. Interview with Lao transport businessman, Houayxay, April 14, 2008.
9. Siriluk, "Sino-Thai Strategic Development," 307; the new travel time estimate is based on two trips undertaken by the authors as well as interviews with Lao taxi drivers.
10. Interview with Chiang Khong Deputy Mayor Tirayudh.
11. "Construction of a New Thai-Lao Friendship Bridge."

12. Interview with anonymous Lao businessperson, June 28, 2008.
13. Erika Fry, "Placing Bets on Luang Namtha," *Bangkok Post*, April 13, 2008, http://www.bangkokpost.com.
14. Interview with three Lao villagers in "new" Boten town, June 28, 2008.
15. Interview with Chinese businessman in "new" Boten town, June 28, 2008.
16. See Fry, "Placing Bets on Luang Namtha."
17. Sirivanh Khontaphane, Sathanbandith Insisiangmay, and Vantana Nolintha, "Impact of Border Trade in Local Livelihoods: Lao-China Border Trade in Luang Namtha and Oudomxay Provinces," Technical Background Paper for the third National Human Development Report, International Trade and Human Development (Vientiane: United Nations Development Program, 2006), 17.
18. Authors' observations and interviews in Boten, April 28, 2008.
19. Interview with Royal Jinlun Hotel's general manager, quoted in Pascale Nivelle, "Lao Vegas," *Quotidien*, April 17, 2007, http://www.liberation.fr/transversales/grandsangles/248001.FR.php.
20. Fry, "Placing Bets on Luang Namtha."
21. Interview with an anonymous casino-room owner, Jinlun Hotel, Golden Boten City, Laos, June 28, 2008.
22. Sirivanh et al., "Impact of Border Trade in Local Livelihoods," 17.
23. Nivelle, "Lao Vegas."
24. William Boot, "Gambling on Lawlessness," *Irrawaddy*, December 30, 2006, http://www.globalgamingnews.com/news_asia/thai-golden-triangle.html; Desmond Ball, "Security Developments in the Thailand-Burma Borderlands," Working Paper no. 9, Australian Mekong Resource Centre, University of Sydney, October 2003; Robert Horn, "Bad Boys Abound in 'Vegas East,'" *Time Magazine*, July 24, 2000, http://www.time.com/time/asia/magazine/2000/0724/thailand.casinos.html.
25. "Mongla Casinos Doomed but That's No Big Deal," Burma News International, March 12, 2008, http://www.bnionline.net/index.php?option=com_content&task=view&id=3745&Itemid=6.
26. Nivelle, "Lao Vegas."
27. Authors' observations.
28. Nivelle, "Lao Vegas."
29. Nivelle, "Lao Vegas"; personal observation.
30. One casino owner at Jinlun Hotel told us that there have been numerous casino-related killings in Boten.
31. Songpol Kaopatumtip and Siriporn Sachamuneewongse, "Shaking up the Neighborhood," *Bangkok Post*, May 4, 2008, http://www.bangkokpost.com.
32. "A Route to Prosperity," *Bangkok Post*, March 29, 2008, http://www.bangkokpost.com.
33. Quoted in Fuller, "Kunming-Bangkok."
34. Interview with Lao villagers in "new" Boten town.

35. Asian Development Bank, "Loan-1989 LAO: Greater Mekong Subregion: Northern Economic Corridor Project". See also ADB loan-related documents including "Report and Recommendation of the President (RRP: LAO 34321, November 2002)."
36. Quoted in Fuller, "Kunming-Bangkok."
37. Fuller, "Kunming-Bangkok."
38. "Highways Prompt Social and Enviornmental Concerns," *Australian Broadcasting Corporation*, April 1, 2008.
39. Quoted in Fuller, "Kunming-Bangkok."
40. David Fullbrook, "Thailand in China's Embrace," *Asia Times Online*, April 9, 2004, http://www.atimes.com/atimes/Southeast_Asia/FD09Ae04.html.
41. Interview with Chiang Khong Deputy Mayor Tirayudh.

Chapter 7: Chiang Saen

1. "Golden Triangle Tax-Free Trading Zone Planned," *Irrawaddy*, July 4, 2006, http://www.irrawaddymedia.com.
2. Saksit Meesukwang, "Thailand in Accord with Burma over Timber Imports," *Chiang Mai Mail*, January 14–20, 2006, http://www.chiangmai-mail.com/169/news.shtml#hd4.
3. "Chiang Saen Port, Thailand's Gateway to Southern China," Chiang Saen Port, PAT, March 22, 2008.
4. "Sino-Thai Trade Needs Improved Logistics," *Bangkok Post*, September 14, 2006, http://www.bangkokpost.com.
5. Kannika Kunakornvaroj, "Rise of Trade Development in Mekong River: A Zero–sum Game?", *Thansettakij*, September 12, 2007, http://www.immf.or.th/articles/Rise_of_Trade_Development.aspx.
6. "Chiang Saen Port, Thailand's Gateway to Southern China," PAT, Chiang Saen Port, March 22, 2008.
7. Theerawat Khamthita, "Heavy Rains Boost Mekong Border Trade," *Bangkok Post*, October 12, 2007, http://www.bangkokpost.com.
8. Interview with Chiang Saen Port spokesman; "Chiang Saen Port, Thailand's Gateway to Southern China."
9. Theerawat, "Transport Mekong River Shipping," *Bangkok Post*, June 5, 2006, http://www.bangkokpost.com.
10. Vaudine England, "Trade Turns Mekong into a River of Plenty," *International Herald Tribune*, July 5, 2006, http://www.iht.com. The reporter quotes the source for these figures as researchers working under the Indochina Media Memorial Foundation in Chiang Mai.
11. Chiang Saen customs chief Patcharadit Sinsawasdi, quoted in "Mekong Drastically Dry," *Bangkok Post*, April 2, 2007, http://www.bangkokpost.com.

12. Songpol Kaopatumtip and Siriporn Sachamuneewongse, "Shaking up the Neighborhood," *Bangkok Post*, May 4, 2008, http://www.bangkokpost.com.

13. Theerawat, "Heavy Rains Boost Mekong Border Trade;" "The Second Port in Chiang Saen District of Chiang Rai," Government Public Relations Department, October 24, 2007, http://www.thailand.prd.go.th.

14. "Northern Ports to be Developed," *The Nation*, July 11, 2006, http://www.nationmultimedia.com.

15. "Chiang Saen Port," a presentation by Phaiboon Phodee, Engineering Department, Port Authority of Thailand, 2008.

16. "The Second Port in Chiang Saen District of Chiang Rai."

17. Chiang Saen Port," 13.

18. Interview with Kesuda Sangkhakorn, Chiang Saen businesswomen and Chiang Saen representative of the Chiang Rai Chamber of Commerce, November 10, 2007.

19. "The Second Chiang Saen Port," insert in "Chiang Saen Port, Thailand's Gateway to Southern China," Chiang Saen Port, PAT, March 22, 2008.

20. "The Second Port in Chiang Saen District of Chiang Rai."

21. Theerawat Khamthita and Amornrat Mahitthirook, "Minister to Push for New Chiang Saen Port," *Bangkok Post*, http://www.bangkokpost.com.

22. Quoted in "Border Trade at Chiang Saen Expected to Boom," *Chiang Mai Mail*, March 6, 2007, http://www.chiangmai-mail.com.

23. "7 Billion ThB Passes through Chiang Saen Customs House in Four Months," *Chiang Mai Mail*, March 4–10, 2006, http://www.chiangmai-mail.com/176/news.shtml#hd18.

24. "Import Quotas for Thai Rubber," *The Nation*, September 14, 2006, http://www.nationmultimedia.com.

25. Cheewin Sattha, "67,000 Tonnes of Dried Longan to be Examined: Bid to Keep Stale Fruit out of Exports to China," *The Nation*, October 12, 2007, http://www.nationmultimedia.com.

26. Soonruth Bunyamanee, "Companies from Yunnan to Build Industrial Estate: Chiang Rai Site to Accommodate Inflow," *Bangkok Post*, December 9, 2003, http://www.bangkokpost.com.

27. Chinese and Thai investors have established the Siam South China Logistics Company, which will construct a port for ships transporting containers on the Mekong. Bannop Tangsriwong and Akekarat Bangleng, "New Silk Road II: China Makes its Mark," *Thai Asia Today*, December 21, 2007, http://www.Thaiasiatoday.com.

28. Theerawat, "Transport Mekong River Shipping."

29. "Mekong River and Burma: China's Two Plans for Secure Energy Transportation," *The Shwe Gas Bulletin*, February 2007, 1.

30. "Chiang Saen Port," 9.

31. Interview with Prathan Inseeyong, Siam South China Logistics, March 2009.

32. "As the River Traffic Dies, Chiang Rai MPs Oppose Dams and New Port," *Chiang Mai Mail*, June 11–17, 2005.

33. Naowarat Suksamran, "Mekong Drastically Dry," *Bangkok Post*, April 2, 2007, http://www.bangkokpost.com.

34. Poona Antaseeda, "Upstream Power Play," *Bangkok Post*, December 22, 2002, http://www.bangkokpost.com.

35. Interview with Kesuda Sangkhakorn.

36. "Chiang Saen Port," 3.

37. Theerawat, "Heavy Rains Boost Mekong Border Trade."

38. See http://www.dams.org/commission/intro.htm.

39. Chatrudee Theparat, "Drying Mekong Worries Tour Firms," *Bangkok Post*, April 14, 2007, http://www.bangkokpost.com; Theerawat Khamthita and Amornrat Mahitthirook, "Minister to Push for New Chiang Saen Port," *Bangkok Post*, http://www.bangkokpost.com.

40. Interview with Kesuda Sangkhakorn.

41. Thein Swe, "The Role of Chiang Mai and Kunming in the Development of the Greater Mekong Subregion," paper presented at the KUST-Payap University Workshop, Kunming University of Science and Technology, Kunming, June 14, 2004.

42. Ibid.

43. England, "Trade Turns Mekong into a River of Plenty."

44. Cited in "Lost in Statistics," *Bangkok Post*, Sunday Perspectives, August 13, 2006, http://www.bangkokpost.com.

45. Quoted in Larry Jagan, "Chinese Food Makes Thais Uneasy," *Asia Times Online*, February 10, 2006, http://www.atimesonline.com.

46. "Thai Troops Asked to Mobilize to Stop Underground Garlic," *Earth Times*, May 7, 2008, http://www.earthtimes.org/articles/show/203698,thai-troops-asked-to-mobilize-to-stop-undergroundgarlic.html.

47. Songpol Kaopatumtip and Siriporn Sachamuneewongse, "Shaking up the Neighborhood," *Bangkok Post*, May 4, 2008, http://www.bangkokpost.com.

48. Interview with Thanasaen Heamaturin, Chiang Saen Customs Office head, March 28, 2008.

49. Interview with Pattana Sitthisombat, Chairman of the Chiang Rai Chamber of Commerce, June 11, 2007.

50. Interview with anonymous Chiang Saen customs officials, March 1, 2009.

51. See Theerawat Khamthita, "New Port for Golden Triangle," *Bangkok Post*, November 19, 2007, http://www.bangkokpost.com; interview with Kesuda Sangkhakorn.

52. From an interview with Pankhae Chunnanond, Deputy Director-General, Business Administration, Port Authority of Thailand, "PAT to Hold a Seminar to Boost Trade Logistics Cooperation among GMS Countries," *Port's News*, PAT, March 2008, 2.

53. "Golden Triangle Tax-Free Trading Zone Planned," *Irrawaddy*, July 4, 2006, http://www.irrawaddymedia.com.

54. Theerawat, "New Private Port for Golden Triangle."

55. Theerawat Khamthita, "Troops to Stop Visits to Burmese Casino," *Bangkok Post*, June 25, 2000, http://wwwbangkokpost.com.

56. Supradit Kanwanich, "Gamblers will Gamble," *Bangkok Post*, 10 November 2002, http://www.bangkokpost.com.

57. Interview with Prathan Inseeyong, Siam South China Logistics, March 2009.

58. Theerawat, "New Private Port for Golden Triangle."

59. Watcharapong Thongrung, "Airport's Luck could Turn," *The Nation*, February 7, 2008, http://www.nationmultimedia.com.

60. Atcha Piyatanang, "Tourism: Chiang Rai Keen to Link Cable Cars to 3 States," *The Nation*, http://www.nationmultimedia.com.

61. Quoted in Robert Horn, "Bad Boys Abound in 'Vegas East,'" *Time Magazine*, July 24, 2000, vol. 156, no. 3, http://www.time.com/time/asia/magazine/2000/0724/thailand.casinos.html.

Chapter 8: Chiang Rai Province

1. Bertil Lintner, "The Golden Triangle Opium Trade: An Overview," *Asia Pacific Media Services*, 2000, http://www.asiapacificms.com/papers/pdf/gt_opium_trade.pdf.

2. David Fulbrook, "Bumpy Road to Thai-China Trade Efficiency," *Asia Times Online*, April 8, 2004, http://www.atimes.online.com.

3. Bannop Tangsriwong and Akekarat Bangleng, "New Silk Road II: China Makes its Mark," *Thai Asia Today*, December 21, 2007, http://www.Thaiasiatoday.com.

4. *Lanna Newspaper* (in Thai), December 25, 2007–March 24, 2008, 6.

5. Bannop Tangsriwong and Akekarat Bangleng, "New Silk Road: A Red Tape Challenge," *Thai Asia Today*, December 10, 2007, http://www.Thaiasiatoday.com (republished from *Phoodjakarn Magazine*).

6. Sasithorn Ongdee, "Plea to Cut Border Charges," *The Nation*, October 9, 2007, http://www.nationmultimedia.com.

7. Sasithorn, "Plea to Cut Border Charges."

8. "Incoming Government Urged to Focus on New Trade Route with China," *The Nation*, January 9, 2008, http://www.nationmultimedia.com.

9. On the Mekong, China, Laos, and Myanmar "have similarly been assigned strategic ports for river trade: China's Mekong trade ports include Simao, Jinghong, Menghan, and Guanlei; for Laos, they are Ban Sai, Xingkok, Mouangmom, Ban Khouane, Houayxay, and Luang Prabang; and in Myanmar, the ports are at Wang Seng and Wan Pong. See "Chiang Saen Port, Thailand's Gateway to Southern China," Port Authority of Thailand, Chiang Saen Port, March 22, 2008.

10. "GMS Development Matrix, Greater Mekong Sub-region, Asian Development Bank, 2008," http://www.adb.org/GMS/Projects/devmatrix.asp?fl=1.

11. "Roundtable/Special Economic Zones: Concern Grows over Impact," *Bangkok Post*, April 11, 2005, http://www.bangkokpost.com.

12. "Current Economic Conditions and Impacts on Thailand and Northern Region," presentation by Warangkana Imudom, Team Executive, Bank of Thailand, Northern Region Office, at Payap University, Chiang Mai, March 12, 2009.

13. National Economic and Social Development Board (NESDB), Gross Regional and Provincial Products 2007.

14. Songpol Kaopatumtip and Siriporn Sachamuneewongse, "Shaking up the Neighborhood," *Bangkok Post*, May 4, 2008, http://www.bangkokpost.com.

15. David Fullbrook, "Thailand in China's Embrace," *Asia Times Online*, April 9, 2004, http://www.atimes.online.com.

16. Interview with Somchai Sirisujin.

17. Songpol and Siriporn, "Shaking up the Neighborhood."

18. Peerawat Jariyasombat, "Road to Yunnan," *Bangkok Post*, May 22, 2008, http://www.bangkokpost.com.

19. Fullbrook, "Thailand in China's Embrace."

20. Bannop and Akekarat, "New Silk Road."

21. Ibid.

22. "A Route to Prosperity: The R3A Highway Holds Plenty of Promise," *Bangkok Post*, March 29, 2008, http://www.bangkokpost.com.

23. Bannop and Akekarat, "New Silk Road."

24. Quoted in Bannop and Akekarat, "New Silk Road."

25. Though customs procedures would be expedited as a result of such harmonization, such changes might also enable transnational corporations (TNCs) to misdeclare the value of goods being transshipped and thus engage in transfer pricing to evade taxes. Such concerns have been reflected in the World Trade Organization (WTO) as well as the United Nations Conference on Trade and Development (UNCTAD). UNCTAD has particularly emphasized the adoption by TNCs of uniform International Financial Reporting Standards. See UNCTAD, *International Accounting and Reporting Issues, 2006 Review*, http://www.unctad.org.

26. "A Route to Prosperity: The R3A Highway Holds Plenty of Promise, *Bangkok Post*, March 29, 2008, http://www.bangkokpost.com.

27. "Roundtable/Special Economic Zones: Concern Grows over Impact," *Bangkok Post*, April 11, 2005, http://www.bangkokpost.com.

28. Fullbrook, "Thailand in China's Embrace."

29. Interview with Pattana Sittisombat, February 22, 2008.

30. Interview with Pattana Sittisombat, April 20, 2007.

31. Interview with Somchai Sirisujin, Chiang Mai Chamber of Commerce, June 10, 2008.

32. Tourism Authority of Thailand, "Internal Tourism in Chiang Mai," and "Internal Tourism in Chiang Rai," Tourism Statistics, http://www2.tat.or.th/stat/web/

static_tst.php; Ministry of Tourism and Sports Statistics, "Accommodation Arrivals of Tourist Attraction in Thailand," 2008 data, http://203.144.250.243/ statistics/otd_acc_est_tour_att_detail.php.

Chapter 9: Chiang Mai

1. The Chiang Mai Metropolitan population was 968,678 in 2008 (including eight inner *amphoe* (districts) of Chiang Mai Province: Mueng Chiang Mai 241,825; San Sai 112,487; Mae Rim 84,815; San Pa Tong 75,923; Saraphi 75,892; San Kamphaeng 76,124; Hang Dong 75,619; Doi Saket 65,810 and two districts of Mueang Lamphun 142,682, and Ban Thi 17,501 in Lamphun Province. Statistics from the Department of Provincial Administration, Ministry of Interior, Thailand.

2. It is difficult to be certain of these figures because only registered inhabitants are counted; sources quickly become out-of-date; and the method by which figures were obtained is not revealed by the sources. Figures are from National Statistical Office of Thailand, *Population and Housing Census 2000*, http://web.nso.go.th/ pop2000/pop_e2000.htm; "Thailand: Largest Cities and Towns and Statistics of their Population," 2008, *World Gazetteer*, http://world-gazetteer.com/wg.php?x =&men=gcis&lng=en&des=gamelan&dat=200&geo=-3&srt=pnan&col=aoh dqcfbeimg&geo=-208; Department of Provincial Administration, Ministry of Interior, Royal Thai Government, http://www.dopa.go.th/; an approximation of 700,000 people living in metropolitan Chiang Mai was quoted in http://www. chiangmailifestyle.com/chiangmai.html.

3. Gustavo Ribeiro and Angunthip Srisuwan, "Urban Development Discourses, Environmental Management and Public Participation: The Case of the Mae Kha Canal in Chiang Mai, Thailand," *Environment and Urbanization* 17, no. 1 (2005): 171, http://www.eau.sagepub.com/cgi/content/abstract/17/1/171.

4. Jim Glassman and Chris Sneddon, "Chiang Mai and Khon Kaen as Growth Poles: Regional Industrial Development in Thailand and its Implications for Urban Sustainability," *Annals of the American Academy of Political and Social Science* 590, no. 1 (2003): 93–115. See also Jim Glassman, *Thailand at the Margins: Internationalization of the State and the Transformation of Labour* (Oxford: Oxford University Press, 2004).

5. Interview with Somchai Sirisujin, Chiang Mai Chamber of Commerce, June 10, 2008.

6. NESDB, Gross Regional and Provincial Products 2007, http://www.nesdb.go.th/ Default.aspx?tabid=96.

7. Figures are from 2005; Chiang Mai Province Website, http://www.chiangmaipoc. net/webeng/#.

8. Ibid.

9. Ibid.

10. Interview with Somchai Sirisujin.

11. Interview with Ratanaporn Sethakul, July 3, 2008.

12. Interview with Somchai Sirisujin.

13. Figures are from 2005; http://www.chiangmaipoc.net/webeng/#.

14. Ibid.

15. Interview with Somchai Sirisujin.

16. Figures are from 2005; http://www.chiangmaipoc.net/webeng/#.

17. See Chayyan Vaddhanaphutti, "The Thai State and Ethnic Minorities: From Assimilation to Selective Integration," in *Ethnic Conflicts in Southeast Asia*, edited by Kusuma Snitwongse and W. Scott Thompson, 151–66 (Singapore: ISEAS, 2005).

18. The new fleet of twenty-six buses would be eco-friendly (running on bio-diesel fuel) and low-cost for passengers. Yet the passenger pick-up trucks (*songtaew*) that have long "maintained a monopoly on Chiang Mai's transportation system" have fretted that these buses will diminish their profits. As such, the Lanna Transport Cooperative, representing the *songtaew* drivers, have alleged that the buses would take passengers from the latter, greatly diminishing the income of the close to 3,000 *songtaew* drivers in Chiang Mai. Due to pressure from the *songtaew* drivers, the new bus system has been slow to get up and running. See Atsadaporn Kamthai, "Chiang Mai Bus Service Delayed," *The Nation*, May 12, 2005, http://www.nationmultimedia.com.

19. Nopniwat Krailerg, "A Report on the Activities of the Chiang Mai Chamber of Commerce in 2005," *Chiang Mai Mail*, March 18–24, 2006, http://www.chiangmai-mail.com/178/news.shtml#hd8.

20. "Locals Lobby PM for a Convention Center," *Chiang Mai Mail*, May 29–June 4, 2007, http://www.chiangmai-mail.com/223/news.shtml.

21. Interview with Somchai Sirisujin.

22. Ibid.

23. Ibid.

24. http://www.visit-chiangmai.com, March 13, 2009.

25. Umesh Pandey, "Dutch Investment Group Ecc Sees Potential for its Destination Malls in Thailand and Vietnam", *Bangkok Post*, Business Section, May 9, 2009.

Chapter 10: Political Decentralization and the Border Trade Thailand

1. This is a growing literature in Thai studies on various aspects of decentralization. See, for example, Michael Nelson, *Central Authority and Local Democratization in Thailand: A Case Study from Chachoengsao Province* (Bangkok: White Lotus Press, 1998).

2. Andrew Walker, "Regional Trade in Northwest Laos: An Initial Assessment of the Economic Quadrangle," in Grant Evans, Christopher Hutton, and Kuah Khun

Eng, *Where China Meets Southeast Asia: Social and Cultural Change in the Border Regions* (Singapore: ISEAS, 2000), 129.

3. Asian Development Bank, *Country Assistance Plan: Thailand 2001–2003* (Manila: 2000), http://www.adb.org/documents/caps/THA/.

4. Anek Laothamatas, *Business Associations and the New Political Economy of Thailand: From Bureaucratic Polity to Liberal Corporatism* (Boulder, Co: Westview Press, 1992).

5. Interview with Somchai Sirisujin, March 22, 2007.

6. Quoted in Vaudine England, "Rising Tide of Trade," *Weekly Standard*, China's Business Newspaper, August 27–28, 2005, http://www.thestandard.com.hk/stdn/std/Weekend/GH27Jp02.html.

7. Interview with Chiang Khong's deputy mayor Tirayudh, June 11, 2007.

8. Interview with Goods Depot Coordinator, Mae Sai, Thailand, July 21, 2007.

9. Interview with Tirayudh, June 11, 2007.

10. Interview with Tirayudh, June 11, 2006.

11. Cambodian Development Research Institute (CDRI), "Thailand's Cross Border Economy: A Case Study of Sa Keo and Chiang Rai," In *Four Country Report*, 2005, www.rockmekong.org/pubs/Year2005/CDRI/FourCountryReport/CDRI_Chapter4_Thailand.pdf.

Chapter 11: Frontier Commerce and Sociolinguistic Challenges in Thailand

1. Interview with Mekong Lao restaurant manager, Houayxay, Laos, June 27, 2008.

2. Cited in Pamaree Surakiat, "The Role of Civil Society in the Promotion and Strengthening of Language Skills of Migrant Workers from Burma: A Case Study at DEAR Burma Project, Bangkok, Thailand," a paper presented at the International Conference on National Language Policy, July 4–5, 2008.

3. Amnesty International, "Thailand: The Plight of Burmese Migrant Workers," Index No. ASA 39/001/2005. http://www.amnesty.org/en/library/info/ASA39/001/2005, January 9, 2005.

4. Songpol Kaopatumtip and Siriporn Sachamuneewongse, "Shaking up the Neighborhood," *Bangkok Post*, May 4, 2008, http://www.bangkokpost.com.

5. Interview with Ratanaporn Sethakul, July 3, 2008.

6. Arunee Wiriyachitra, "English Language Teaching and Learning in Thailand in this Decade," 2001, http://www.apecneted.org/resources/downloads/English%20Language%20Teaching%20and%20Learning%20in%20Thailand.pdf.

7. Anucha Charoenpo, "Prime Ministers Open New Highway to China," *Bangkok Post*, http://www.bangkokpost.com.

8. "New Batch of Chinese Language Teachers Arrives in Thailand," June 2, 2008, The Office of Chinese Language Council International, Government of China, http://www.hanban.org/en_hanban/content.php?id=3294.

Conclusion

1. For asymmetrical interdependence in borderland areas, see Oscar J. Martinez, "The Dynamics of Border Interaction: New Approaches to Border Analysis," in *Global Boundaries, World Boundaries*, vol. I, edited by C. H. Schofield, 1–15 (London: Routledge, 1994).

2. Liu Jinxin and Xiong Bin, "Strategic Development of Logistics Cooperation between Yunnan, China and Northern Thailand," paper presented at the "Logistics Development in the Greater Mekong Sub-region Conference," March 18–19, 2008, US Commercial Service, Shangri-La Hotel, Chiang Mai, http://www.buyusa.gov/thailand/en/logistics.html.

3. Ibid.

4. Thein Swe, "Myanmar Economic Outlook," in *Regional Outlook, Southeast Asia 2011–2012*, edited by Michael J. Montesano and Lee Poh Onn, 142–51 (Singapore: ISEAS, 2011).

5. Stephen Brooks, "Dueling Realisms," *International Organization* 51, no. 3 (1997): 446.

Bibliography

Abonyi, George. "Activity-Based Regional Cooperation in Asia." Paper prepared for Asian Development Bank workshop, 2003. http://www. adbi.org/files/2003.12.10.cpp.activity.based.cooperation.pdf.

Amnesty International. "Thailand: The Plight of Burmese Migrant Workers." January 9, 2005. Index no. ASA 39/001/2005. http://www.amnesty.org/ en/library/info/ASA39/001/2005.

Anek Laothamatas. *Business Associations and the New Political Economy of Thailand: From Bureaucratic Polity to Liberal Corporatism.* Boulder, Co.: Westview Press and Singapore: ISEAS, 1992.

Anucha Charoenpo. "Prime Ministers Open New Highway to China." *Bangkok Post*, April 1, 2008. http://www.bangkokpost.com.

Arghiros, Daniel. *Democracy, Development and Decentralization in Provincial Thailand.* Richmond: Curzon Press, 2001.

Arunee Wiriyachitra. "English Language Teaching and Learning in Thailand in this Decade," 2001. http://www.apecneted.org/resources/downloads/ English%20Language%20Teaching%20and%20Learning%20in%20 Thailand.pdf.

Asian Development Bank (ADB). "Report and Recommendation of the President to the Board of Directors on a Proposed Loan to the Lao People's Democratic Republic for the Greater Mekong Subregion: Northern Economic Corridor Project." RRP: LAO 34231. Manila: ADB, 1990.

———. *Country Assistance Plan: Thailand 2001–3.* Manila: ADB, 2000. http://www.adb.org/documents/caps/THA/.

———. "Technical Assistance (Financed from the Japan Special Fund) to the Lao People's Democratic Republic for Preparing the Northern Economic Corridor Project." TAR: LAO 34231. Manila: ADB, December 2001. http://www.adb.org/Documents/TARs/LAO/r12_02.pdf.

———. "Report and Recommendation of the President to the Board of Directors on a Proposed Loan to the Lao People's Democratic Republic for

the Greater Mekong Subregion: Northern Economic Corridor Project."
RRP: LAO 34321. Manila: ADB, 2002.

—. "Regional Technical Assistance: The North-South Economic
Corridor: Progress towards a Full-fledged Economic Corridor." RETA:
6310. Manila: ADB, 2006.

—. "GMS Development Matrix, Greater Mekong Sub-region." Manila:
ADB, 2008. http://www.adb.org/GMS/Projects/devmatrix.asp?fl=1.

—. *Key Indicators for Asia and the Pacific 2008*. Manila: ADB, 2008.
http://www.adb.org/statistics.

—. *Outlook 2008 Update*. Manila: ADB, 2008. http://www.adb.org/
Documents/Books/ADO/2008/Update/Part03-VIE.pdf.

Atcha Piyatanang. "Tourism: Chiang Rai Keen to Link Cable Cars to 3 States."
The Nation, August 15, 2004. http://www.nationmultimedia.com.

Atsadaporn Kamthai. "Chiang Mai Bus Service Delayed." *The Nation*, May 12,
2005. http://www.nationmultimedia.com.

Ball, Desmond. "Security Developments in the Thailand-Burma Borderlands."
Working Paper no. 9, Australian Mekong Resource Centre, University of
Sydney, October 2003.

Bannop Tangsriwong and Akekarat Bangleng. "A New Silk Road?" *Thai Asia
Today*, December 10, 2007. http://www.Thaiasiatoday.com.

—. "New Silk Road II: China Makes its Mark." *Thai Asia Today*,
December 21, 2007. http://www.Thaiasiatoday.com.

Barth, Aharon. "Econo-Realism: Putting Economics at Center Stage. How
Does, and Should, IR Research React to Expanding Economic
Interdependence?" Paper presented at the International Studies Association,
41st Annual Convention, Los Angeles, March 14–18, 2000. https://www.
ciaonet.org/isa/baa01/.

Battersby, Paul. "Border Politics and the Broader Politics of Thailand's
International Relations in the 1990s: From Communism to Capitalism."
Pacific Affairs 71, no. 4 (1998–99): 473–88.

Bello, Walden. "China and Southeast Asia: Emerging Problems in an Economic
Relationship." *Transnational Institute*, December, 2006. http://www.tni.
org/archives/act/16053.

Booth, Martin. *Opium: A History*. New York: Thomas Dunne, 1996.

Booth, William. "Gambling on Lawlessness." *Irrawaddy*, December 30, 2006.
http://www.globalgamingnews.com/news_asia/thai-golden-triangle.
html.

Brooks, Stephen. "Dueling Realisms." *International Organization* 51, no. 3 (1997): 445–77.

Central Intelligence Agency (CIA). "Laos". *The World Factbook*, 2010. https://www.cia.gov/library/publications/the-world-factbook/geos/la.html.

Chambers, Paul. "Edgy Amity along the Mekong: Thai-Lao Relations in a Transforming Regional Equilibrium." *Asian Journal of Political Science* 17, no. 1 (2009): 89–118.

———. "Harnessing Suwannaphum: Thailand's Foreign Economic Policy toward Mainland Southeast Asia in the Era of Thaksin." In *Bureaucracy and National Security in Southeast Asia: Essays in Honor of M. Ladd Thomas*, edited by Daniel H. Unger and Clark D. Neher, 131–61. DeKalb: Northern Illinois University Press, 2006.

Chambers, Paul, and Eva Pascal. "Oblique Intervention: The Role of US Missionaries in Siam's Incorporation of Lanna 1867–1878." *Journal of World Christianity* 2, no. 1 (2009): 29–81.

Chatrudee Theparat. "Drying Mekong Worries Tour Firms." *Bangkok Post*, April 14, 2007. http://www.bangkokpost.com.

Chayyan Vaddhanaphutti. "The Thai State and Ethnic Minorities: From Assimilation to Selective Integration." In *Ethnic Conflicts in Southeast Asia*, edited by Kusuma Snitwongse and W. Scott Thompson, 151–66. Singapore: ISEAS, 2005.

Checkel, Jeffrey T. "Social Construction and Integration." Oslo: Advanced Research on the Europeanisation of the Nation-State (ARENA) Working Paper 98/14, 1998.

Cheewin Sattha. "67,000 Tonnes of Dried Longan to be Examined: Bid to Keep Stale Fruit out of Exports to China." *The Nation*, October 12, 2007. http://www.nationmultimedia.com.

Chen Xiangming. *As Borders Bend: Transnational Spaces on the Pacific Rim*. Lanham: Rowman & Littlefield, 2005.

Chinese Government Official Website. "Premier Wen Makes Proposals on Boosting Co-op in GMS." March 31, 2008. http://english.gov.cn/2008-03/31/content_933280.htm.

Chomsky, Noam. *Profit over People: Neo-liberalism and Global Order*. New York: Seven Stories Press, 1999.

Dosch, Jörn. "Managing Security in ASEAN-China Relations: Liberal Peace of Hegemonic Stability." *Asian Perspective* 31, no. 1 (2007): 209–36.

Earth Times. "Thai Troops Asked to Mobilize to Stop Underground Garlic," May 7, 2008. http://www.earthtimes.org/articles/show/203698,thai-troops-asked-to-mobilize-to-stop-underground-garlic.html.

Embassy of the Lao PDR to the United States of America. "Investment Opportunities and Selected Potentially Attractive Sectors." http://www.business-in-asia.com/laos.htm.

England, Vaudine. "Rising Tide of Trade." *Weekly Standard*, August 27–28, 2005. http://www.thestandard.com.hk/stdn/std/Weekend/GH27Jp02.html.

———. "Trade Turns Mekong into a River of Plenty." *International Herald Tribune*, July 5, 2006. http://www.iht.com.

Evans, Grant, Christopher Hutton, and Kuah Khun Eng. *Where China Meets Southeast Asia: Social and Cultural Change in the Border Regions.* Singapore: ISEAS, 2000.

Foucault, Michel. *Power/Knowledge: Selected Interviews and Other Writings, 1992–97.* Edited by C. Gordon. New York: Pantheon, 1980.

Fry, Erika. "Placing Bets on Luang Namtha." *Bangkok Post*, April 13, 2008. http://www.bangkokpost.com.

Fulbrook, David. "Bumpy Road to Thai-China Trade Efficiency." *Asia Times Online*, April 8, 2004. http://www.atimes.com.

———. "Thailand in China's Embrace." *Asia Times Online*, April 9, 2004. http://www.atimes.com.

Fuller, Thomas. "Kunming-Bangkok." *International Herald Tribune*, March 30, 2008. http://www.iht.com.

———. "Notorious Golden Triangle Loses Sway in the Opium Trade," *International Herald Tribune*, September 11, 2007. http://www.iht.com/articles/2007/09/11/asia/golden.php.

Gilpin, Robert. *War and Change in World Politics.* Cambridge: Cambridge University Press, 1981.

Glassman, Jim. "Recovering from Crisis: The Case of Thailand's Spatial Fix." *Economic Geography* 83, no. 4 (2007): 349–70.

———. *Thailand at the Margins: Internationalization of the State and the Transformation of Labour.* Oxford: Oxford University Press, 2004.

Glassman, Jim, and Chris Sneddon. "Chiang Mai and Khon Kaen as Growth Poles: Regional Industrial Development in Thailand and its Implications for Urban Sustainability." *Annals of the American Academy of Political and Social Science* 590, no. 1 (2003): 93–115.

Goodman, David S. G., ed. *China's Campaign to "Open the West": National, Provincial, and Local Perspectives*. Cambridge: *China Quarterly* Special Issue, Cambridge University Press, 2004.

Government Public Relations Department [Thailand]. "Construction of a New Thai-Lao Friendship Bridge," March 16, 2007. http://www.thailand.prd.go.th.

————. "The Second Port in Chiang Saen District of Chiang Rai." October 24, 2007. http://www.thailand.prd.go.th.

Gramsci, Antonio. *Selections from the Prison Notebooks*. Translated and edited by Quintin Hoare and Geoffrey Nowell Smith. New York: International Publishers, 1971.

Guttal, Shalmali. "An Investor's Paradise: Trade in the Mekong Region." *Focus on the Global South*, March 2006. http://www.focusweb.org/an-investor-s-paradise-trade-in-the-mekong-region.html.

————. "Marketing the Mekong: The Asian Development Bank and the Greater Mekong Sub-region Economic Cooperation Program." *Focus on the Global South*, December 12, 2003. http://www.jubileesouth.org.

Haas, Peter M. "Introduction: Epistemic Communities and International Policy Coordination." *International Organization* 46, no. 1 (1992): 1–35.

He Jinsong. "Myanmar Migrant Workers in Thailand: Policies and Prospects." *Asian Scholar* 5 (2007). http://www.asianscholarship.org/asf/ejourn/articles/he_j.pdf.

Hirst, Paul and Grahame Thompson. *Globalization in Question: The International Economy and the Possibilities of Governance*. Cambridge, Mass.: Wiley-Blackwell, 1999.

Hopfner, Jonathan. "Fast Times." *Globe and Mail*, January 10, 2004, T1. http://www.globeandmail.com.

Horn, Robert. "Bad Boys Abound in 'Vegas East.'" *Time Magazine*, July 24, 2000. http://www.time.com/time/asia/magazine/2000/0724/thailand.casinos.html.

Htet Aung. "Thailand Marks Trade Deficit with Burma." *Irrawaddy*, June 18, 2007. http://www.irrawaddymedia.com.

International Organization for Migration (IOM). *Across Borders: Harnessing the Advantages of Migration in Southeast Asia,* 2009. http://www.iom-seasia.org/index.php?module=pagesetter&func=viewpub&tid=6&pid=40.

Jagan, Larry. "Chinese Food Makes Thais Uneasy." *Asia Times Online*, February 10, 2006. http://www.atimes.com.

Kahrl, Fredrich, Su Yufang, and Horst Weyerhaeuser. "Navigating the Border: An Analysis of the China-Myanmar Timber Trade." Washington, D.C.: Forest Trends, 2004.

Kannika Kunakornvaroj. "Rise of Trade Development in Mekong River: A Zero–sum Game?" *Thansettakij*, September 12, 2007. http://www.immf. or.th/articles/Rise_of_Trade_Development.aspx.

Kasikorn Research Centre. "Thailand and Laos: Cooperation Enhancing Mutual Prosperity." March 19, 2004. http://www.kasikornresearch.com.

———. "Vietnam vs. Thailand: Competitors in Trade-Investment-Tourism." May 3, 2006. http://www.kasikornresearch.com/kr/eng/search_detail. jsp?id=5527&cid=11.

Kawasaki, Tsuyoshi. "Post-Classical Realism and Japanese Security Policy." *Pacific Review* 14, no. 2 (2001): 221–40.

Kean, Thomas. "Kyaukphyu-Yunnan Oil Pipeline to be Completed by End of 2015." *Myanmar Times*, November 30–December 6, 2009. http:// mmtimes.com/no499/no13.htm.

Keohane, Robert O. "International Institutions: Two Approaches." *International Studies Quarterly* 32, no. 4 (1988): 379–96.

———. "Neoliberal Institutionalism: A Perspective on World Politics." In *International Institutions and State Power: Essays in International Relations Theory*, edited by Robert Keohane, 1–20. Boulder, Co.: Westview, 1989.

Keohane, Robert O., and Joseph Nye. *Power and Interdependence: World Politics in Transition*. Boston: Little, Brown, 1977.

Kosum Saichon. "ASEAN +3 and GMS: Case Studies of Regional Integration." In *Contemporary Global Issues in Social Sciences*, edited by Usamad Siampakdee. Chiang Mai: Chiang Mai University, 2005.

Kramer, Tom, Martin Jelsma, and Tom Blickman. *Withdrawal Symptoms in the Golden Triangle: A Drugs Market in Disarray*. Amsterdam: Transnational Institute, 2009. http://www.tni.org/report/withdrawal-symptoms-golden-triangle-4.

Kratochwil, Friedrich E., and John Gerard Ruggie. "International Organization: A State of the Art on an Art of the State." *International Organization* 40 (1986): 753–75.

Kuah Khun Eng. "Negotiating Policies: Border Trading in Southern China." In *Where China Meets Southeast Asia: Social and Cultural Change in the Border Regions*, edited by Grant Evans et. al, 72–97. Singapore: ISEAS, 2000.

Lahu National Development Organization. "Aftershocks along Burma's Mekong." *Burma Library*, September 5, 2003, http://burmalibrary.org/docs/AFTERSHOCKS%20ALONG%20BURMA.htm.

———. "Road Construction in Shan State: A Lucrative Way to Turn Illegal Drug Profits into Legal Revenues." *Undercurrents: Monitoring Development on Burma's Mekong*, January 2005. http://www.burmariversnetwork.org/burmese/images/stories/publications/english/undercurrents1.pdf.

Lintner, Bertil. "The Golden Triangle Opium Trade: An Overview." Asia Pacific Media Services, 2000. http://www.asiapacificms.com/papers/pdf/gt_opium_trade.pdf.

Liu Jinxin and Xiong Bin. "Strategic Development of Logistics Cooperation between Yunnan, China and Northern Thailand." Paper presented at the Logistics Development in the Greater Mekong Sub-region Conference, US Commercial Service, Shangri-la Hotel, Chiang Mai, March 18–19, 2008. http://www.buyusa.gov/thailand/en/logistics.html.

Martinez, Oscar J. "The Dynamics of Border Interaction: New Approaches to Border Analysis." In *Global Boundaries, World Boundaries*, vol. I, edited by C. H. Schofield, 1–15. London: Routledge, 1994.

Marx, Karl. *Capital: An Abridged Edition*. Edited by David McLellan. Oxford: Oxford Paperbacks, 2008.

McCoy, Alfred. "Requiem for a Drug Lord: State and Commodity in the Career of Khun Sa." In *States and Illegal Practices*, edited by Josiah McC. Heyman, 129–68. Oxford: Berg, 1999.

McCoy, Alfred, Cathleen Reed, and Leonard Adams. *The Politics of Heroin in Southeast Asia*. New York: Harper and Row, 1989.

Mekong River Commission (MRC). *The People's Highway: Past, Present and Future Transport on the Mekong River System*. Vientiane: MRC Secretariat, 2003.

Mergawati Zulfakar. "ASEAN Charter Inked." *The Star*, November 20, 2007.

Mittleman, James. "Rethinking the International Division of Labour in the Context of Globalisation." *Third World Quarterly* 16, no. 2 (1995): 273–95.

Murphy, Craig. "Freezing the North-South Bloc(k) after the East-West Thaw." *Socialist Review* 20, no. 3 (1990): 25–46.

———. *Global Institutions, Marginalization, and Development*. London: Routledge/RIPE Studies in Global Political Economy, 2005.

Mutebi, Alex. "Recentralising while Decentralising: Centre-Local Relations and 'CEO' Governors in Thailand." *Asia-Pacific Journal of Public Administration* 26, no. 1 (2004): 33–53.

Naowarat Suksamran. "Mekong Drastically Dry." *Bangkok Post*, April 2, 2007. http://www.bangkokpost.com.

———. "New Thai-Lao Bridge Throws up Old Problems." *Bangkok Post*, April 23, 2007. http://www.bangkokpost.com.

Naowarat Suksamran and Subin Kheunkaew. "A Bridge Too Far: Many Local Residents Are Still Not Convinced the Project Will Take Off." *Bangkok Post*, February 18, 2007. http://www.bangkokpost.com.

National Statistical Office of Thailand. *Population and Housing Census 2000*. http://web.nso.go.th/pop2000/pop_e2000.htm.

Nelson, Michael. *Central Authority and Local Democratization in Thailand: A Case Study from Chachoengsao Province*. Bangkok: White Lotus, 1998.

———. "Thailand: Problems with Decentralization?" In *Thailand's New Politics: KPI Yearbook 2001*, edited by Michael H. Nelson, 219–81. Nonthaburi and Bangkok: King Prajadhipok's Institute and White Lotus Press, 2002.

———. "Analyzing Provincial Political Structures in Thailand: *phuak, trakun*, and *hua khanaen*." Southeast Asia Research Centre Working Paper no. 78. Hong Kong: City University of Hong Kong, 2005. http://www.cityu.edu.hk/searc.

Nivelle, Pascale. "Lao Vegas." *Quotidien*, April 17, 2007. http://www.liberation.fr/transversales/grandsangles/248001.FR.php.

Nopniwat Krailerg. "A Report on the Activities of the Chiang Mai Chamber of Commerce in 2005." *Chiang Mai Mail*, March 18–24, 2006. http://www.chiangmai-mail.com/178/news.shtml#hd8.

Oehlers, Alfred. "A Critique of ADB Policies toward the Greater Mekong Sub-region." *Journal of Contemporary Asia* 36, no. 4 (2006): 464–79.

Office of Chinese Language Council International, Government of China. "New Batch of Chinese Language Teachers Arrives in Thailand [in Chinese]." June 2, 2008, http://www.hanban.org/en_hanban/content.php?id=3294.

Ohmae, Kenichi. *The Borderless World: Power and Strategy in the Interlinked Economy*. New York: HarperBusiness, 1990.

———. *The End of the Nation State: The Rise of Regional Economies*. New York: Free Press, 1995.

———. *The Next Global Stage: Challenges and Opportunities in Our Borderless World*. Upper Saddle River, NJ: Wharton, 2005.

Pamaree Surakiat. "The Role of Civil Society in the Promotion and Strengthening of Language Skills of Migrant Workers from Burma: A Case

Study at DEAR Burma Project, Bangkok, Thailand." Paper presented at the International Conference on National Language Policy, Bangkok, July 4–5, 2008.

Pandey, Umesh. "Dutch Investment Group ECC Sees Potential for its Destination Malls in Thailand and Vietnam." *Bangkok Post*, May 9, 2009. http://www.bangkokpost.com.

Parker, Clive. "Straining to Bridge the Divide." *Irrawaddy*, February 10, 2006, http://www.irrawaddy.org/aviewer.asp?a=5451&z=104.

Pathan, Don. "Greater Mekong Subregion Moves Closer." *The Nation*, July 5, 2005, http://www.nationmultimedia.com.

Peerawat Jariyasombat. "Road to Yunnan." *Bangkok Post*, May 22, 2008. http://www.bangkokpost.com.

Petchanet Patruangkrai. "Non-Tariff Barriers with China Attacked." *The Nation*, May 26, 2007. http://www.nationmultimedia.com.

Phaiboon Phodee. "Chiang Saen Port." Presentation, Engineering Department, Port Authority of Thailand, 2008.

Pholsena, Vatthana, and Ruth Banomyong. *Laos: From Buffer State to Crossroads?* Chiang Mai: Mekong Press, 2006.

Poona Antaseeda. "Upstream Power Play." *Bangkok Post*, December 22, 2002. http://www.bangkokpost.com.

Porametee Vimolsiri. "Thailand as a Transport Hub for the Greater Mekong Subregion." NESDB, 2007. http://www.nesdb.go.th-Portals-0-home-interest-Thailand as a Transport Hub.pdf.

Port Authority of Thailand (PAT). "Chiang Saen Port: Thailand's Gateway to Southern China." *Port's News*, March 22, 2008.

———. "PAT to Hold a Seminar to Boost Trade Logistics Cooperation among GMS Countries." *Port's News*, March 2008.

———. "The Second Chiang Saen Port." Insert in "Chiang Saen Port: Thailand's Gateway to Southern China." *Port's News*, March 22, 2008.

Purba, Mandala Sukarto. "Towards Regionalism through the ASEAN-China Free Trade Area: Prospects and Challenges." Master's Thesis, University of the West Cape, May 2006. http://etd.uwc.ac.za/usrfiles/modules/etd/docs/etd_gen8Srv25Nme4_9213_1183461348.pdf.

Quadrelli, Roberta. "ASEAN Statistics by the International Energy Agency." Paper presented at the Training Session on Emergency Preparedness and Statistics, Paris, February 11–14, 2008. http://www.iea.org/work/2008/asean_training/Quadrelli.pdf.

Ramsay, Ansil. "Modernization and Reactionary Rebellions in Northern Siam." *Journal of Asian Studies* 38, no. 2 (1979): 283–97.

Ribeiro, Gustavo and Angunthip Srisuwan. "Urban Development Discourses, Environmental Management and Public Participation: The Case of the Mae Kha Canal in Chiang Mai, Thailand." *Environment and Urbanization* 17 (2005): 171–182.

Rose, Gideon. "Neoclassical Realism and Theories of Foreign Policy." *World Politics* 51, no. 1 (1998): 144–72.

Saccardo, Nadia. "China: Targeted for In-Bound FDI," *Business-in-Asia*, 2005. http://www.Business-in-Asia.com.

Sai Soe Win Latt. "What if Thailand Wants 'Migrant Problems?'" *Irrawaddy*, July 14, 2008. http://www.irrawaddy.org/opinion_story.php?art_id=13315.

Saksit Meesubkwang. "As the River Dies, Chiang Rai MPs Oppose Dams and New Port." *Chiang Mai Mail*, June 11–17, 2005. http://www.chiangmai-mail.com.

———. "Thailand in Accord with Burma over Timber Imports." *Chiang Mai Mail*, January 14–20, 2006. http://www.chiangmai-mail.com/169/news.shtml#hd4.

———. "Burmese Authorities Permit Teak Imports." *Chiang Mai Mail*, August 19–25, 2006. http://www.chiangmai-mail.com/200/news.shtml#hd9.

Sasithorn Ongdee. "Plea to Cut Border Charges." *The Nation*, October 9, 2007. http://www.nationmultimedia.com.

Shwe Gas Bulletin. "Mekong River and Burma: China's Two Plans for Secure Energy Transportation," February 2007.

Siriluk Masviriyakul. "Sino-Thai Strategic Development in the Greater Mekong Subregion (1992–2003)." *Contemporary Southeast Asia* 26, no. 2 (2004): 302–20.

Sirivanh Khontaphane, Sathanbandith Insisiangmay, and Vantana Nolintha. "Impact of Border Trade in Local Livelihoods: Lao-China Border Trade in Luang Namtha and Oudomxay Provinces." Technical Background Paper for the third National Human Development Report, International Trade and Human Development. Vientiane: United Nations Development Program, 2006.

Somphong Wanapha. "The Shifting Paradigm of FDI Policy and Promotion in Thailand." Paper presented at the Global Forum on International Investment: Attracting Foreign Investment for Development. Organization for Economic Cooperation and Development (OECD), Shanghai, December 5–6, 2002. http://www.oecd.org/dataoecd/54/63/2764564.pdf.

Son, Johanna. "Open Borders Expose Mekong's Disparities." *IPS News*, February 10, 2007. http://www.ipsnews.net/news.

Songpol Kaopatumtip and Siriporn Sachamuneewongse. "Shaking up the Neighborhood." *Bangkok Post*, May 4, 2008. http://www.bangkokpost.com.

Soonruth Bunyamanee. "Companies from Yunnan to Build Industrial Estate: Chiang Rai Site to Accommodate Inflow." *Bangkok Post*, December 9, 2003. http://www.bangkokpost.com.

Sopaporn Saeung. "Second Bridge to Burma Opens in Mae Sai." *The Nation*, January 23, 2006. http://www.nationmultimedia.com.

Sundaram, Meenakshi S. S. *Decentralisation in Developing Countries*. New Delhi: Concept Publishing, 1994.

Supradit Kanwanich. "Gamblers will Gamble." *Bangkok Post*, 10 November 2002. http://www.bangkokpost.com.

Sutheera Atawongsa. "Guidelines for Development of Border Trade between Thailand and Southern China: A Case Study of Chiang Saen District." Thesis abstract, Faculty of Management Sciences, Chiang Rai Rajabhat University, 2006. In *CRU Post*, Special ed., 35th anniversary, 2007. http://www.cru.in.th.

Tanit Sorat. "Thailand Cross Border Logistics." Paper presented at the Logistics Development in the Greater Mekong Sub-region Conference, US Commercial Service, Shangri-La Hotel, Chiang Mai, March 18–19, 2008. http://www.buyusa.gov/thailand/en/logistics.html.

Taran, Patrick, and Eduardo Geronimi. "Globalization, Labor and Migration: Protection is Paramount." Paper presented at the Conferencia Hemisférica sobre Migración Internacional: Derechos Humanos y Trata de Personas en las Américas, Santiago de Chile, November 20–22, 2002.

Theerawat Khamthita. "Troops to Stop Visits to Burmese Casino." *Bangkok Post*, June 25, 2000. http://wwwbangkokpost.com.

———. "From Chiang Rai to China via Burma: New Transnational Road Due for Completion within Two Weeks." *Bangkok Post*, January 14, 2004. http://www.bangkokpost.com.

———. "Industrial Estate Move Confirmed." *Bangkok Post*, January 12, 2005. http://www.bangkokpost.com.

———. "Heavy Rains Boost Mekong Border Trade." *Bangkok Post*, October 12, 2007. http://www.bangkokpost.com.

———. "New Private Port for Golden Triangle." *Bangkok Post*, November 19, 2007. http://www.bangkokpost.com.

Theerawat Khamthita and Amornrat Mahitthirook. "Minister to Push for New Chiang Saen Port." *Bangkok Post*, June 2, 2008, http://www.bangkokpost.com.

Thein Swe. "The Role of Chiang Mai and Kunming in the Development of the Greater Mekong Subregion." Paper presented at the KUST-Payap University Workshop, Kunming University of Science and Technology, Kunming, June 14, 2004.

————. "Myanmar Economic Outlook." In *Regional Outlook: Southeast Asia 2011–2012*, edited by Michael J. Montesano and Lee Poh Onn, 142–51. Singapore: ISEAS, 2011.

Thein Swe and Paul Chambers. "Political Economy on the Perimeter: State Policy and Trade on Thailand's Border with Myanmar and Lao PDR." Paper presented at the 10th International Thai Studies Conference, Thammasat University, Bangkok, January 9–11, 2008.

Tourism Authority of Thailand. "Tourism Statistics." http://www2.tat.or.th/stat/web/static_tst.php.

Trento, Joseph J. *The Secret History of the CIA*. New York: Carroll and Graf, 2005.

Tsuneishi, Takao. "The Regional Development Policy of Thailand and its Economic Cooperation with Neighboring Countries." Institute of Developing Economies (IDE) Discussion Paper no. 32. Chiba: IDE-JETRO, 2005.

————. "Thailand's Economic Cooperation with Neighboring Countries and its Effects on Economic Development within Thailand." IDE Discussion Paper no. 115. Chiba: IDE-JETRO, 2007.

United Nations. *Human Security Report 2005*. New York: United Nations, 2006. http://www.humansecurityreport.info/.

United Nations Conference on Trade and Development (UNCTAD). *International Accounting and Reporting Issues, 2006 Review*. http://www.unctad.org.

United Nations Economic and Social Commission for Asia and the Pacific (UNESCAP). *Greater Mekong Subregion Business Handbook*. New York: United Nations, 2002.

————. "Trade Facilitation in the Greater Mekong Subregion." In *Trade and Investment Division Report 2007*. http://www.unescap.org/tid/publication/chap9_2224.pdf.

Viotti, Paul, and Mark Kauppi. *International Relations Theory: Realism, Pluralism, Globalism, and Beyond*. Third ed. Boston: Allyn and Bacon, 1999.

Walker, Andrew. *The Legend of the Golden Boat: Regulation, Trade and Traders in the Borderlands of Laos, Thailand, China, and Burma.* Honolulu: University of Hawai'i Press, 1999.

———. "Regional Trade in Northwestern Laos: An Initial Assessment of the Economic Triangle." In *Where China Meets Southeast Asia: Social and Cultural Change in the Border Regions,* edited by Grant Evans, Christopher Hutton, and Kuah Khun Eng, 122–24. Singapore: ISEAS, 2000.

———. "A Flood of Chinese Garlic." *New Mandala: New Perspectives on Mainland Southeast Asia* (blog), October 24, 2007. http://asiapacific.anu. edu.au/newmandala/2007/10/24/a-flood-of-chinese-garlic/.

Wallerstein, Immanuel. "Patterns and Perspectives of the Capitalist World Economy." *Contemporary Marxism* 9 (1984): 59–70.

———. *The Modern World-System: Capitalist Agriculture and the Origins of the European World-Economy in the Sixteenth Century.* New York: Academic Press, 1976.

Walt, Stephen. "International Relations: One World, Many Theories." Special Edition, "Frontiers of Knowledge," *Foreign Policy* 110 (1998): 29–46.

Waltz, Kenneth. *Theory of International Politics.* New York: McGraw-Hill, 1979.

———. "Realist Thought and Neorealist Theory." *Journal of International Affairs* 44, no. 1 (1990): 21–38.

Warangkana Imudom. "Current Economic Conditions and Impacts on Thailand and Northern Region." Presentation, Bank of Thailand, Northern Region Office, at Payap University, Chiang Mai, March 12, 2009.

Watcharapong Thongrung. "Airport's Luck could Turn." *The Nation,* February 7, 2008. http://www.nationmultimedia.com.

Wendt, Alexander. "Collective Identity Formation and the International State." *American Political Science Review* 88, no. 2 (1994): 384–96.

Wichit Chaitrong. "Mekong States Meet on Customs." *The Nation,* September 15, 2006, http://www.nationmultimedia.com.

Wilson, Constance M. "The Holy Man in the History of Thailand and Laos." *Journal of Southeast Asian Studies* 28, no. 2 (1997): 345–64.

World Bank. *Lao Economic Monitor,* 2006. http://lnweb18.worldbank.org/ eap/eap.nsf/Attachments/LaoPDR+EcMonitor0403/$File/LaoPDR+ EcMon0403.pdf.

World Gazetteer. "Thailand: Largest Cities and Towns and Statistics of their Population," 2008. http://world-gazetteer.com/wg.php?x=&men=gcis&l ng=en&des=wg&srt=npan&col=abcdefghinoq&msz=1500&geo=-208.

Yongyuth Chalamwong, Worawan Chandoewit, and Srawooth Paitoonpong. "Thailand's Cross Border Economy: A Case Study of Sa Keo and Chiang Rai." *Four Country Report*. Phnom Penh: Cambodian Development Research Institute (CDRI), 2005. http://www.rockmekong.org/pubs/Year2005/CDRI/FourCountryReport/CDRI_Chapter4_Thailand.pdf.

Yuan Fu Yang, Bryant. "Life and Death away from the Golden Land: The Plight of Burmese Migrant Workers in Thailand." *Thailand Law Journal* 1, no. 12 (Spring 2009). http://www.thailawforum.com/Volume12Spring%2009.html.

Index